The Jesus Purpose

The Jesus Purpose

Born to Die, Created to Live

William Thrasher

ISBN: 978-0-9970386-0-6
Library of Congress Control number: 2016905350

10 9 8 7 6 5 4 3 2 0 4 1 3 1 6

Printed in the United States of America

♾ This paper meets the requirements of ANSI/NISO Z39.48-1992 (Permanence of Paper)

Cover painting by Marlan Yoder
Cover painting photographed by Tom Mileshko Photography

"I've told you these things for a purpose: that my joy might be your joy, and your joy wholly mature. This is my command: Love one another the way I loved you. This is the very best way to love."

-Jesus of Nazareth

CONTENTS

ACKNOWLEDGMENTS

IT IS WITH HEART-FILLED GRATITUDE THAT I RECOGNIZE the following people for their help and support through the development process of this book.

To our church family at His Hands, you opened your doors and hearts and provided a place of love and grace, thank you. To our friends who have prayed and invested for and with us, thank you.

To my gang of twelve who I asked to take time and energy to read and respond to my first draft, thank you. To my coworkers and business partners, for an environment to provide an ability to work on this in tandem with our daily tasks, thank you.

To our outstanding publishing team for the hard work and belief in this project, thank you. To our cover art partners, Marlan and Tom, for the creativity and generosity, thank you. To my spiritual coaches and idea sounding boards, Justin and Ben, thank you.

To my parents, Bill and Suzy, and my sister Annie, for continuous support, prayer, and encouragement, thank you. To my other parents, Leland and Denise, and sisters Michelle and Jennifer, for making me a true part of your family, thank you. To my kids, Will and Ainsleigh, for your hugs, kind hearts, and inspiration, thank you.

To my gorgeous and amazing wife, Kristina, for an earthly partnership of love, joy, and grace beyond what I could have ever imagined, thank you.

To my Creator, savior, and lover of my soul, I could never say thank you enough.

***

To each of you, I truly love you all.

INTRODUCTION

ONE SEEMINGLY UNEVENTFUL MORNING I SAT QUIETLY sipping coffee and reflecting on what had just transpired. The last week had been one of the most eventful and life-altering weeks of my life. My wife of fourteen years had undergone brain surgery to resolve a miraculously discovered aneurysm. This thirty-six-year-old mother of two was certain that she would not awaken after the procedure. Thankfully, she did.

As I relaxed in our living room's purple recliner, a hand-me-down piece of furniture that she had elegantly blended into our home décor, my thoughts drifted from the recent past to the more distant future. I began to identify trends and markers that, when meditated upon, showed a remarkable picture. Were these personal grid points of history—cause and effect, choices made, crossroads taken—more than a simple series of random chance happenings? Could I take time, focus, and prayer to introspectively chart my personal journey and see what was possibly in store for my future? What value would such an exercise produce?

In the stillness of patience, waiting through the process of healing to overtake my bride, I came to this spirit-lifting revelation:

> *My blessings are infinite, my planning will always be insufficient, but it is still necessary. His plan is complete and working toward a perfect Kingdom—but I can only catch a small glimpse of His plan in fractions of moments, forever moving forward without pause.*
>
> *I'm sitting alone, working from home today while Kristina rests, trying to gain wisdom on what best to focus on for my part in that perfect plan.*
>
> *It's exciting, confusing, humbling, and requires a patience I'm not very good at.*
>
> *Today I look forward. By knowing where I've been and where I am, I hope to better focus my blessings, energy, and joy toward a small series of new goals, and to pursue them with the revitalized passion and purpose of a completely forgiven US Marine who's being told to charge a new hill . . .*

I wrote these words on a simple Facebook status update. The commentary from friends and family was quite interesting in the day or so afterwards. Many sent messages of hope and comfort. A few saw joy and rejoiced with a perspective of inspiration. Yet others simply understood my limited ability to draw such insight; these few saw this as divine revelation.

That morning was the beginning of this book.

I'm not anyone who would be highlighted as "special" from a broad sociological perspective. I live in a typical house, I had a blessed and balanced upbringing, I have a wonderful career, and I enjoy my provisional living. I have amazing friends and family and a beautiful partner in marriage. I believe you would meet me and very likely think, "He's a nice guy, a regular guy who's not perfect and doesn't try to be, and he sure loves life."

I would have to agree with that assessment . . . That's exactly who I am.

The question it poses: Why?

The simple, yet transforming answer will be repeated throughout the chapters of this book. It is not something that can be adopted in a quick session of reading. It is a lifelong process that has proven to provide a worth beyond the worldly tangible.

Some skeptics will criticize the following philosophy as a process-oriented scheme of biochemistry; an organically-cultivated framework which, via a naturally dependent process, forced our early ancestors to seek unsolvable answers from myth, rather than fact. Through such organic processes they believe that mankind was forced to develop morality, consciousness, and law to prolong our evolutionary survival and quality of living.

Others may blast the forthcoming ideas as myopic and hate-filled; blaming the messenger for pointing to a path that delivers true peace down a road less traveled—a road that was constructed as far back as written record can take us, a road that navigates anyone's life-hope to a single conduit.

Can a single path provide such fulfillment for anyone?

The simplicity of this life's purpose will be found in a final moment.

You will not live, as you do now, forever.

It's a harsh and chilling reckoning that every living, self-aware creature must face. Upon such realization and in the very fractions of moments when such imminent certainty sets in, final truth will be revealed.

There are only two possible outcomes that can follow death:

Complete Revelation or Absolute Nothingness.

You were born to die.

The answer we all hope to find through the heartbeats that follow our formation, the answer this book hopes to guide you toward is this:

You were created to live.

CHAPTER 1

THE WAY, THE TRUTH, THE LIFE

JESUS OF NAZARETH WAS BORN ROUGHLY 2,000 YEARS ago. His physical existence as a real person on this planet is rarely questioned and easily testable. We know through historical records that he lived a relatively simple life for many of his thirty-three years and dynamically changed the culture of civilization upon his death.

There are collections of personal accounts and letters that describe Jesus and his philosophical thoughts, his eventful actions, and his relational experiences. Collections of these texts have been processed through more than any other documentation ever. Arguments over credibility, value, accuracy, intent, and agenda can be found in all forms and fashions. The theological and anthological perspectives that can be reviewed are easily accessible in this day of information saturation. Seeking out such information about the who, what, where, and how of Jesus would merely be a complementary exercise to what this book hopes to reveal. This book is simply about the *why*.

Why is Jesus so important? The firsthand words by and works about Jesus are likely the most studied passages of literature ever recorded. Why has his message transcended the bounds of history, culture, technology, and terrain? Why do countless people—intellectuals or simpletons, leaders or followers, royalty or peasants, hopeful or hopeless—all find comfort and peace from a Jewish carpenter who was routinely executed by local authorities?

What this flesh-and-blood human named Jesus offers is an alternative from the rights and wrongs of man, an answer to consciousness, and an anticipation beyond basic mortality.

The religious label assigned to those following the teachings of Jesus is "Christianity." Denominations are groups of likeminded followers who have basic agreement with their personal interpretations of Biblical texts. Hierarchy, structure, conformity, and tradition are the frameworks of the modern church. Collective individuals gather to perform orchestrated sessions of public worship, teaching, and fellowship. This model of church has provided society with a very encapsulating image of what it means to be a follower of Jesus.

Stereotypes abound. You know them well, whether you're a Christian or not; your mind can list the common characteristics of the typical "Bible Believer." The mental images we conjure of regular churchgoers and enthusiastic evangelical zealots, while diverging, permeate through and past the point of what Jesus said and did. These stigmas have a tendency to distract and taint. These labels bring up discomfort and uncertainty as to whether digging into the heart of Jesus's life and teachings is worthwhile.

In an ironic and subjective parallel, there is another counterproduct of the church and a communal Jesus following: Conformance Pressure. For many people, it's simply easier to be a "Christian" than not. Who really wants to trudge through the social dogma of counterculture? Life is simply easier to walk and talk when we do as others do.

You know . . .

. . . to go about and passively put on your best clothing during the first day of each week; to open your hymnal to page 135 and sing stanzas one, two, and four; to get some practical and wise advice about an area of life; to grab a lunch out at the local Mexican restaurant with good friends; to nap watching some routine sporting event; maybe wash the car; prepare for the next week ahead. Lather, rinse, repeat.

Is that all Jesus has to offer? If so, the Christian faith is the most pathetic religion ever developed and it is destined for nurturing only the drab, the insane, and/or the lemming.

Thankfully, that is far from what Jesus offers. The above routine is the by-product of religious association. Jesus hated religion's effects.

Jesus was raised in a hyper-religious culture, a distant descendant from a bloodline of nobility, expected to know how and what to do at all times. He grew up in a small town outside of the epicenter of his natural-born religion. He became intimate with the inner workings of the synagogue and temple, and he personally observed oppressive rule from both political- and faith-labeled authorities.

The majority of his recorded life focuses on a period of public calling.

Jesus spent what is generally accepted as three years sharing a unique, counterintuitive wisdom, performing unexplainable acts of healing and wonder, and befriending a group of select men to whom he shared a personal partnership and friendship with. During this small window of time, he set the foundation for an extreme shift in human culture. In what would seem to be a preplanned process—aligning thousands of years of documented history, prophecy, and predictions—this one man's life would forever offer an alternative to our seemingly natural callings, offering a purpose beyond ourselves.

Jesus would claim he is our life's purpose and his existence on earth is to pursue you. This bold proclamation would be the eventual reasoning behind his death. Despite the hype and perceived supernatural feats that followed this common Middle Easterner, he otherwise had nothing revealing that should have made him special. On what grounds did this person have the right to claim such egotistical, authoritative, invasively disturbing nonsense?

Jesus's life, death, and post-death appearances are either the most elaborate and well-coordinated acts of deception or a calling for an exploration of faith. That's the first and only step we're asked to take. Can you, at a minimum, objectively step back—throw out the stereotypes, ditch the conformity, set aside the religion—and ask yourself, why? Why Jesus?

Now, this book comes with a guarantee. This book will highlight the path to purpose, perspective, and peace for your one-chance life. But it involves work in order to have this guarantee pay off. However, to give such a guarantee cannot come from some undereducated author . . . Sorry to disappoint. Such a guarantee must come from that which ***Will Be*.**

The guarantee is simply this: Follow Jesus and he will provide you the way, he will always provide you with truth, and through a lifelong process he will give you an abundant fulfillment of purpose in life.

This path isn't about rules or regulations—it's about a journey of *real life*, in a real existence, with real results.

CHAPTER 2

REAL LIFE

YOU MIGHT HAVE NOTICED THAT SO FAR, I HAVE YET to directly quote from the Bible. Yep—that's right. If you're looking for that, there are tons of great resources out there to help you navigate the personal adventure ahead.

This book is more like a compass. A compass cannot tell you where to go, what road to take, or how far to travel. It is merely a tool to help point you in the needed direction.

The outcome of this journey, should you so be inspired, is to test the direction ahead.

Yes—test. Question, hypothesize, plan, implement, adjust, prove, disprove, fail, succeed, and most importantly, share the results.

There is no formula for living life. The subconscious, involuntary parts of being will continue until they don't. You awaken after rest. You breathe, you sense, you move . . . those happen regardless of choice. Everything else has at least a small component of conscious selection. Like it or not, that's truth, and right at this moment, you're choosing to accept that mind-blowing notion. Cool, huh?

Involved in this finite existence are four accessible dimensions: height, depth, width, and time. We only can be aware of items that are directly related to a relationship of cause and effect. All we can imagine, do, or calculate is a by-product of this closed environment.

Good and bad are personal perspectives based on your discrete point of view. They are wholly subjective and only exist in the self-aware space that we call our minds. Deep stuff, I know—but we're setting the stage for a really awesome way to approach everything you have and will come to experience.

Your mind is made of inert materials in a perfect combination of bonded connections processing encoded energy pulses. Your thoughts, feelings, and awareness are completely made from things that pose no living qualities at all. In fact, the sheer concept of life, outside of the fact that it just exists, is beyond all scientific calculation or understanding. There will never be any viable explanation of how that which has life came to be from the known materials and energy that are inert. We can observe and measure the effects and results, but the *why* answers will always be what adverts the valiant seeker who is searching only in the observable and measurable, physical existence.

In the most basic of scientific truth, you are made from light. The beginning of all time and existence came from an unexplained cause. This is a simple, yet unfathomable fact to ponder. When considered in full context of seeking truth, it brings us to a point we are often uncomfortable with. We love answers. We like to <u>*know*</u> what we believe has assured validity.

This is where we generally lay our foundations for building personal convictions; where we find unifying and comforting solace. For many people, those foundations are set in a heavy backing of scientific research and well-tested evidence. For others, it may exist among the company and beliefs of social associations such as faith groups. Others find peace of mind in an existence and assurance free from any defined purpose or calling.

Regardless of the perspective you have, you exist, you are aware, and you can ask the question, "Why?"

When you come to know what you are and that you really should not exist as you do, you can instantaneously recognize that you are indeed special. Yes, that sounds epically cliché, and in terms of historical existence of all life you're one of billions, perhaps trillions, of organic mechanisms—hardly a blip on the cosmic radar. But it's simply true. Your "fingerprint" will never exist again. You are completely distinct and nothing can ever replicate you. No one will ever have your point of view, your set of experiences, or your opportunities for choice.

If you merely ask the natural question of why to that testable fact, it is beyond tragic to have the elementary response of "because." In its essence, "Be Caused" has purpose: You were created to have effect, make impact. Therefore, the very answer to even the non-answer is purpose. You *were* caused for a purpose. We can therefore say you were created for a purpose.

Now, toning down the philosophy a good bit, where does this fit into a daily routine?

The process of living can become repetitive and wearing over time. How much different would your point of view be if you knew, beyond all doubt, that everything about you was filled with purpose? What if you could begin to dial in the coordinates to provide a path to follow? A path which leads to a life of greater perspective, ultimate joy, and complete fulfillment—a path of purpose with an identifiable objective? What would you give to have that voyage each and every day?

This road is available to you. It cannot be earned or bought. You cannot force your way onto it with a process or procedure. No amount of random wandering will provide you with direction onto it . . . What it requires is a choice.

Yes, back to that conscious decision to act. The only way you can walk this amazing path of growth and enlightenment is to follow. Follow not a what, but rather, a who.

You don't have to change anything to begin. It doesn't matter where you are or what you have done. You simply make a willing choice to begin a simple walk, one step at a time with Jesus.

This is not about finding religion; this is about testing a personal offer. The value as described earlier cannot be measured or objectified. It's not necessarily a path of ease or luxury, but it will provide more joy than can ever be measured, and leads to an outcome that makes all things work together in a harmonious relationship of balance and perfect resolution.

This path, should you begin, can be abandoned at any time should the claims above not be delivered on. That is the guarantee.

It is a test . . . AND, it is a gift. You have done nothing to deserve this opportunity.

CHAPTER 3

ACCEPTING PURPOSE

IMAGINE YOU ARE GIVEN AN IMPOSSIBLE, BUT UNavoidable, test to pass. You have a time limit and you have open-book resources, but there are countless distractions, and failure holds a disastrous outcome.

Buried inside of every solvable equation on the test lies a clue. No matter how well you excel, you cannot pass this test. Your only hope for getting through this required course is to garner enough information from clues to find a very simple secret. The only way to overcome this test is to provide the professor with your name and resign yourself that your efforts are insufficient—his mercy is the only hope of passing.

This above scenario is very similar to how our Creator, the one who caused everything, the installer of purpose, designed us to live.

You are programmed to strive for more than the test allows on its surface review. You are wired to ask why. This universe and its entire splendor point like a giant blinking arrow toward something bigger. The Book of Genesis highlights this fact and gives sole credit to one it labels as God. God is the causal agent of everything, as mentioned in the previous chapter.

In our classroom environment, God parallels the professor. This existence is His realm of purpose and planning. How He did it can be weighted and measured. When He did it can be calculated. Where we fit has its framework. But *why* He did it . . . well, that requires thought, reasoning, and most importantly, a component of faith to find and trust what truth ***Will Be***.

If you can get to a point where you find it reasonable that a Creator exists—a supernatural being responsible for all existence—then, you must also give that deity credit for life and this creation's associated purpose, regardless of understanding it thoroughly.

The God of Genesis' creation takes His credit via a first chapter, a poetic narrative beginning with all time and space. Through repetitive periods of forming order from chaos, He takes complete credit for this universe and earth filled with miraculous life. The theology of this text can be taken and processed through all sorts of filters and approaches, but the big picture point being made is this: ***There is a causal agent and It is responsible for everything that exists.***

So no matter how we come to identify these clues, through a process of scientific research or via the search for divine disclosure, we ultimately arrive at the same endpoint: God holds the key to your purpose.

So if existence in itself points to a Creator God as its cause, and this Creator God holds the answers to our life's reason, where does Creator God point us?

This Creator has pointed all design, tactfully guided all history, and crafted every heart and mind to the sole purpose of that Jewish carpenter named Jesus. Just like you, Jesus was born to die. Jesus's purpose was to give you life. Your created purpose is to receive that final and simple truth.

The testing process of this life will move forward from where you are right now toward the inevitability of its final moment of responsiveness. The clues ahead might be crystal clear at times or they might be buried under deep layers of sediment. As a self-aware being, you're under a constant pull toward finding a longing purpose. The process of pursuing truth will strengthen and solidify your understanding as you begin to walk with Jesus.

The more you grow in knowledge of His plan and ways, the more you're drawn to the conclusion there is nothing you can do which can give you more than what He gives to you freely. This is the paradox of life.

You find associations to it in many philosophical teachings or alternative religious perspectives, but to journey with Jesus is the essence and resolution of this reverse-logic offering from God.

To receive is to give.

The more you give, the more you receive.

Jesus asks you to give up everything materially desired and simply follow him. In doing so, he offers a promise to give you more than you can ever imagine.

This is not something you can calculate or process. It can only be experienced. Through experience, it can be revalued and invested. Then, it can be grown into a thriving relationship of trust, honor, and grace. Those key characteristics will then invade your very core and build the foundational structure of the intangible quality we identify as love.

This lifelong test will provide challenges, trials, rewards, and produce passion. It will prove sustainable through the easiest and most difficult of situations, growing more strengthened with each forward step.

The Creator gave us His purpose. It is not for a rational or conventional mind to solve and it cannot be overcome with human ingenuity or intelligence. Men and women are called to it constantly. We can get close to finding it on our own, but to find Jesus is to unveil the ultimate purpose of life.

To follow Jesus, with open and free willingness, is to accept the purpose of life.

CHAPTER 4

BUCKET LIST

ORGANIZATION IS A COMMON TRAIT OF THE SUCCESSFUL. By managing how we divide and store what we are responsible for, one can become systematic and find a comfortable process which provides structure to your surrounding environment. You are built as a compartmentalization machine. You are made of three equal, combined, but unique parts. For the purposes of this book, we will define them as such:

Body, Mind, and Spirit.

Depending on context, the word "soul" is often interchangeable in the above descriptions for either Mind or Spirit. Here, for clarification's sake, I will stick to the above trifecta.

The Body is easy to understand. It is the physical and tangible matter of you: your hair, skin, bones, and blood—it is the three-dimensional self you experience the universe through.

The Mind is also a fairly easy concept to rationalize. Your mind is "who" you are: your thoughts, your emotions, your memories, your personality. It is the processor which translates all the sensory experiences from your body, develops patterns based on a collection of information over time, and develops understandings based on that collected information.

The Spirit is the toughest by far to define or recognize. Your spirit is what sets you apart from any other living thing that has ever existed. Your spirit is the fashioned conduit which channels the intangible and immeasurable. Art, music, poetry, romance, engineering, philosophy, and self-awareness are all uniquely human traits that would not naturally come from some undirected process. Your spirit is what longs to ask for purpose and yearns to seek answers to the incomprehensible.

Each of these "buckets" were designed to symbiotically thrive off of each other. You were created by a set of plans that were already in existence.

The author of Genesis identified this set of plans as the "Image of God." Like you, the God of creation reveals Himself through three equal, combined, but unique parts. For the purposes of this book we will define them as such: Jesus (Son), Creator (Father), and Spirit (Holy Spirit).

This design is the image that you were fashioned after. Jesus was a real person—he is the Body in the design plan for you. Jesus is the physical, material, tangible, testable component of God. The Creator is wisdom without cause, the Mind in the design plan for you. The Creator offers the vison, plan, personality, and emotional heart of the unseen but ever-active component of God. Just as the Spirit is the toughest part of defining or recognizing for you and me, so as it is with God. God's spirit is what gave you the gift that sets you apart from any other living thing that has ever existed. This Spirit is your transceiver, which offers access to all that is intangible and immeasurable. This Spirit is what provides us a conduit to individually connect with our Creator and find purpose in this independent life we journey.

Developing an understanding of how you are built and how you are compartmentalized helps you then focus on where you are affected when life is in constant transition. This God-reflected model of symbiotic facets allows us to experience our existence through both the physical world we sense, and also through realms beyond that which can be measured or fully understood. Our reasoning minds appear to be overly compensated to things that would matter little to an existence based solely on survival. The creativity and passions of humanity lend themselves to a deistic quality that allows us to become the creators of our own worlds and ideas.

Your physical makeup is the tool that allows this unexplainable mutation to thrive in an ever-changing environment of decay and what can only be described as a seemingly unmanageable, chaotic universe. Yet here you are, doing just that.

While we can all sit and process that you have little control of what is big, it is equally as recognizable that you have a vast and direct ability to control who and where you are and what you think—all of which lends back into the effects of this uncontrollable, universal creation. It's a dichotomy that only one with a spiritual outlook can truly find to be beautiful. Otherwise, this is a cruel accident, void of hope or purpose.

You exist in these three parts, and each of them is vital to having balance in this life. They must each be nourished and maintained properly, in equal and appropriate fashion, to find peace on this earth amidst this chaotic existence. Finding this peace requires more than you alone can provide. This process is highlighted by example in children. The more advanced the life-form, the more attention that is required to develop and grow the corresponding offspring. In the case of humanity, an investment of roughly twenty-five years is required to achieve full physical development.

This process cannot be fulfilled without the necessary relationship of a parenting partner. You are born requiring help to survive. You are born needing constant attention to grow and maturate. It is not a debatable point—we as people are created to require help.

This process of growth at the guiding and assisting hands of others, to whom you are wholly dependent, is easily identified in our physical (Body) and mental (Mind) facets. The Spirit is no different. It requires help to grow into a mature state. It needs constant nourishment and maintenance to reach its full and valuable potential, just like the rest of you.

Chapter 5

Work It Out

A couple of years ago I came to a moment of realization with myself: I was getting fat. No beating around the bush—I was at a very clear crossroads. I had always been a lean guy who maintained a high metabolic rate; I could eat whatever I wanted and still felt physically confident in my abilities to do almost anything. This startling revelation rocked and changed my blinded perspective based on history, rather than present truth.

I had always vowed never to get out of shape. I grew up in a house where members of my family had battled weight wars on a revolving basis. I saw the firsthand results of how genetics combined with diet and exercise can lead to lifelong struggles against obesity and healthiness. It not only produced a physical toll, but the paralleled emotional and social abuse was also evident and active. The attention needed to resolve such an uphill fight was all-encompassing.

I swore my life would be different.

Such circumstances are easily relatable for many people. We have all looked in a mirror or at a test result and harbored a deep-down disappointment in what is looking back at you. There is no one to point fingers at—ownership for this situation can only be focused back introspectively.

It's easy to have a misaligned perspective of personal fitness. What you are and where you have come from, progress through the narrow-minded gaze of your small world; a world that has repeatedly fed you false interpretations of reality. This produces a localized experience based on choices made, reactions taken, and plans made from that recycling myopic point of view.

Two of the biggest falsehoods indoctrinated into our society that play havoc with our personal well-beings are:

- ***Everyone*** is created equal
- You aren't good enough, and you ***need*** to be better

Neither of these statements holds up to any rational thought, yet almost all personal stress circles back to one of these two illogical perspectives.

Addressing the first falsehood, everyone is NOT created equal. In fact, everyone is created ***uniquely***! The misunderstanding to this untruth involves a subtle, but detrimental, shift in transposing how a government or institution should view and judge its associated people versus how we individually react and relate to interpersonal relationships, including the relationship you have with yourself.

We are not all equal and you will never be uniformly equal to anyone, ever. Who you are is completely special in that regard, and how you are made is equally true. To compare any individual person to another instantly begins a process that will highlight the obvious differences in strengths and weaknesses. That process is natural and normal. It's an objective part of how we relate to the living world around us, but when we attempt to filter those differences through any definition of what "equal" should represent personally, only suffering can follow.

Addressing the second falsehood, "You are not good enough, and need to be better." The irrationality is apparent from the start. There is a vital, but impossible variable to define, a component completely missing from the statement, a necessary value which determines the thresholds of good and better.

Who or what determines those bounds? If there are any identifiable markers in this existence, as we experience it, how can anyone possibly be certain they have achieved those minimal objectives necessary for peace or balance, enlightenment, or fulfillment? What is good enough? What is better enough? Where or what is that line and who controls it?

Such a lie is impossible to escape! It as well can only deliver hopelessness.

So, if those are lies, what is true?

- ***You are special and you always have room to grow.***

This simple perspective shift can radically change how you approach everything you interact with. You are no longer responsible for achieving based on external markers, but rather have an expectation to adapt and personally evolve in every moment that approaches.

Each experience and every interaction is a part of who you are becoming, how you are growing, and what personal levels of peace and fitness you hold.

You now change based on internal factors. You make calculated decisions to personally mature and become fit based on personal potential and your uniqueness. Your goals and objectives shift to manageable steps, and your exercise routine becomes part of growth rather than a process to become something or someone you were not created to be.

You become you . . . with every emergent indication of who you ***Will Be***.

CHAPTER 6

THE OBJECTIVES OF EXERCISE

AFTER THIS PERSONAL AWAKENING TO THE FACT THAT I was quickly becoming out of shape physically, I decided that I needed to make a serious and conscious effort to become more fit. I knew the steps I needed to take and how long such a process can take. Most importantly, I also knew how much time, energy, and effort are needed to simply maintain the reasonable goals I had set once I got there. Once at my goals, it would take constant maintenance to sustain the fitness levels that I had worked so hard to achieve.

In order to know where to set my goals, I needed a target, an objective. I needed something to challenge myself against, to see if I had achieved my goals in the time frame set and to create a motivation for upkeep beyond.

In that same year, I committed and paid to run the Tough Mudder, a twelve-and-a-half-mile obstacle course designed by a British Special Forces veteran. The course challenges the areas of endurance, strength, and sheer will.

I had set before me a six-month plan to shed my excess and strengthen my body . . . and I put cash-money on the line.

I began working out regularly, lifting weights, cardio, running, and preparing in any way to be ready for what was ahead of me. It was exhilarating and exhausting. I was waking up at 4:45 a.m. to train, while dieting, and focusing on being successful at my goals and my specific objective ahead, the Tough Mudder.

The day of the race came. I had prepared well and was physically and mentally ready. The course was easily describable in two obvious words: tough and muddy. I overcame every physical obstacle and challenge with relative ease, running the course faster than I had expected—hardly ever pausing through the twelve and a half miles. It was a fantastic result achieved by setting a clear goal and targeting a specific result.

Exercise is a choice. It's a process to work on something progressively, a conscious decision to strengthen and sustain. Exercise is not limited to the physical, but as a tangible example and paralleling metaphor, it yields great insight.

You exercise to strengthen an area of perceived weakness. You provide repetitious and increasing loads to an area, challenging it to achieve greater efficiency in process. You continuously, and without fail, maintain these areas of built-up strength, otherwise they will become diminished once again over time.

Strength is best achieved by beginning with the core. Starting on a peripheral appendage can garner limited strength, but its value is only as resilient as the core strength allows. In fact, a strong appendage without a strong core can become an area of flaw; unnatural compensation can result in damage to areas which were not meant to hold such loads.

Focus on core strength development is essential to finding your maximum potential, and core strength exercises yield practical and performance-based results. Core strength is the key component of maintaining balance and a foundation to build everything else upon.

Balance is vital to living. Balance is the fine-tuning required for survival. It allows specific and detailed variables to live in perfect coexistence, providing the seemingly unworkable to work together in a harmonious manner. Take sodium and chlorine as examples. Both are toxic to humans in marginal quantities, but, when combined and put into a chemical balance, they become an essential part of what we need to live: NaCl or sodium chloride, best known as table salt.

Balance, when properly achieved, provides a life-giving, comfortable, and joy-enhancing journey. It allows you to move in each moment on a graceful path. This fine-tuned objective is the process in which we were created to live. The universe and all that resides within its dimensional boundaries are carefully and meticulously fine-tuned. All harmonized within a perfect balance of that which is required for—get this—you.

All that is and all that has been inside of this creation sits in a perfect balance for you. At first thought, it may seem like an awful waste of time, energy, and material. Why would the vast and incomprehensible universe be put in place, designed, and all conformed to support you?

That's not an answer we can know. We cannot know the complete why, but we can know truth.

When put into perspective, the cosmos and all that is could never self-produce life without an infinite number of attempts. Life is unexplainable, and its maturation to self-awareness is another statistical impossibility of unguided nature. There is no logic, no reason, no calculation that can explain its causation. It just is.

You were created to be a connected part of that balance. From every part of your physical existence, you are interconnected and interdependent on its being, at the mercy of each moment that exists. Only in the framework of combined Mind and Spirit can you process this concept. That in itself lends credibility to the Creator's image, the reflective picture of who is and who ***Will Be***.

When you begin to embrace this reasoning, it begins the process of exercise for your spirit. It becomes intimately aware that it is not a fatigued or atrophied appendage of self, but rather a source of unlimited power, peace, and purpose.

When combined with physical fitness, mental stimulation, and a spiritual awakening through the love and grace of your Creator's spirit, your form in this existence is made closer to who you are intended to be and will forever become.

CHAPTER 7

THE SHADOWS OF SELF

THERE'S A CONCEPT THAT COMES FROM FOLLOWING Jesus that assures of a life beyond this creation, a new physical place where everything will be recreated and we will exist as we were truly intended. It's a difficult image to dwell upon as the Biblical imagery speaks in metaphors of known factors which can do no justice to the true glory of what is being prepared for you.

Depictions dial in on gates of pearl and streets of gold. Cultural imagery paints a picture of clouds and cherubs, harps and halos, and perhaps a waiting line with a list of hopeful entrants to see if their name might be included in the book that St. Peter holds. We're told there's a river with Trees of Life lining its banks, and there's a room prepared for you, filled with the treasures you've earned (note that this one has always bugged me).

One other important characteristic of this new creation we're told specifically that in God's presence: there ***Will Be*** no shadows.

This is an interesting and unfathomable concept to include in such an ancient work of literature. Shadows give depth to our world. Shadows indicate the direction of light and provide us with vital information on what we are observing. Shadows also offer refuge to that which does not wish to be seen; whether hidden for protection or concealing for deceit. Shadows play an interdependent role in our relationship with this creation.

So I ask you a simple question: What exactly is a shadow?

Webster's Dictionary helps provide the following definition: "an area of darkness created when a source of light is blocked." Darkness is the absence of light. Darkness is nothing. It is a void of emptiness, an unfulfilled potential of space.

We carry around shadows within our own minds, areas of deep regret, sorrow, pain, remorse, anxiety, weakness, anger, jealousy, addiction, fear, and ego. We generally hide these manifestations of life's unfortunate experiences behind the façade of our daily interactions. We shield and bury them deep within until those shadows of emptiness invade into the light-filled spaces and we cannot help for that darkness to surface into the physical.

We often react to the materialization of the darkness through our physical self in outburst; a seemingly uncontrollable rage of emotion and involuntary expulsion of pain. This mental discomfort, not unlike the sense of aches we feel through our physical body, also weakens our abilities and limits potential. Unlike our physical pain, these outbursts of emotion can be redirected and cause direct influence and impact to others; relationships are vulnerable prey of these internal shadow-storms.

This shadowing of self might seem like an unsolvable dilemma of humanity's design; a hopeless trap of our own cognizance; a cruel trick of a demented Creator. I have witnessed the shadows-of-mind destroy lives of self and others. I have observed shadows overtake control and result in irreparable earthly damage. It's impossible to imagine a place without shadows . . . but the hope of such a place is better understood when the definition of the word itself is exposed.

Shadows do not actually exist. They are voids. They are nothing. Shadows are areas of *potential* waiting for light to fill their emptiness and bring into view all that can and ***Will Be***.

There is only one primary source of light in our physical earth: the sun, a G2V-type star, a yellow dwarf positioned at the center of our solar system. A giant fusion reaction sparked from the trails and traces of the universe's inception, an unusually stable source of heat and light for this speck of collected dust we dwell upon. All that we can physically sense is completely dependent on the Sun.

Not unlike the physical, the spiritual part of you needs a source of light. Something to shine its rays of warmth and expose the darkness of the mind that we hold on tightly to; a source of unlimited power, the source of all hope.

In a twist of English irony, we too are completely dependent on the Son to provide this light.

It is not by a power of ego that can enlighten and repair the voids of self-darkness we choose to create. Humanity can attempt in all its worldly, holistic ways to provide this power. It can give an illusion of peace, security, and purpose—but it is just that, a false reality.

Without the Son, darkness within you will always remain.

The pure light provided to our minds when the spirit of the Creator connects to our spirit begins to cast out the voids of darkness in our personal worlds. With investment into the teachings and prophecies of Jesus, we are enlightened to our ultimate purpose and the hope of life's true meaning.

Through prayer, a constant conversation with the living spirit within, the strength of hope is encouraged and vitalized. This process begins to methodically fill our dark emptiness with a living enlightened garden of love, joy, patience, kindness, goodness, faithfulness, gentleness, and self-control. Confidence shifts from self to Son, and the power of all that is and ***Will Be*** provides a peace that surpasses all natural understanding.

Through this, shadows disappear and light begins to permeate the spaces that were intended to flourish and thrive in an eternally focused life. That which was or is pain becomes joy and resolve, overcoming the darkness, filling the emptiness.

The Son, Jesus, gives your world the light of life.

CHAPTER 8

STOCKPILING TREASURE

I BRIEFLY MENTIONED IN THE PREVIOUS CHAPTER A small detail about the prospect of heaven that has always bugged me—treasure. What is that all about? Are we supposed to earn wealth for eternity? We're assured there is no pain, no hurt. We will be part of a perfect existence as we were intended to thrive . . . and there will be *treasure*?!

Treasure is possessive. It directly projects to the material side of our hearts' desires. Treasure has ruled the dreams and conquests of history. It has started world wars and tempted brother to kill brother. It is the root of much of the darkness embedded within humanity . . . and we're going to have it . . . in heaven?!

In the walls of our modern-day church and its curious cultural quirks, I have even heard people comment to its personal allure and perceived accumulation. After doing a deed from a worldly perspective seen as "good," I've heard (in the best Dana Carvey Church Lady voice I can conjure) . . . "You've earned another jewel for your crown in Heaven!"

It always brought to mind a sense of competition . . . and I am a very competitive person. *"So, you're telling me this is a race to see who can earn the most treasure? Well, bring it, because I'm not going to lose!"* This mentality has been used as a persuasive tool of many church environments I have been exposed to. As I came to better know the spirit of Jesus—the exact representation of the Creator, the light who is filling the darkness within my own person—I had an impossible time rationalizing the discrepancy it caused.

I continued to feel empowered by this race of treasure, a race whose by-product was an infinite marathon of hollowness; an empty void of abuse and selfishness, capitalized on by those who claimed to follow the same Jesus of hope I did. Where was truth? Where was the life in this treasure race?

When the spirit of self connected to Christ's spirit is trained, it begins to develop strength. As this process maturates, the voids of darkness are enlightened, and moments of brilliance beyond one's own capacity to articulate can be channeled. In the areas of doubt, uncertainty, and even conflict, we can be provided sparks of amazing revelation.

In the case of my continued internal debate and battle with the purpose of eternity's "treasure," I was provided such a spark. Now, I cannot remember the specific details surrounding the moment when the light of truth filled my void of dark misunderstanding. It was likely while driving on my morning commute or taking a shower; those times are when many of my moments of enlightenment come. But I know it wasn't manifested from within self. This was an unspoken conversation between self and something beyond self.

"Treasure" was inappropriately defined within the shadows of my own mind. It was a developed understanding from the point of view that I had been influenced and indoctrinated with. My perspective was misaligned with this other voice; it was giving me an alternative point of view, a new perspective which was not that of my own experience.

This "treasure" of eternity could not be a source of social measure. It could not be judged as excessive or insufficient. It had no value beyond its pricelessness to its owner. It could not affect feelings of jealousy, conflict, or pride. This treasure had to be of purity, like that which this broken world could not portion, but that only this existence could produce.

This was a true enlightening.

The treasure is our life's journey—all of that which encompasses our path toward an intended relationship with our Creator. The joys of moments vividly remembered and those tucked away in the shadows alike are no longer hidden from the perspective of the myopic self. Rather, they ***Will Be*** revealed to see how they fit wholly and purposefully in their perfect place. A personal wealth of all of life's moments was now revealed through a new filter of unrelenting love and grace and purpose.

Hope from this angle begins to overtake one's perspective on life in an overwhelming manner. The light of the Son, connected through his Spirit to ours, changes the understanding and shifts the outcomes and decisions for the future. It's a simultaneously improvised and choreographed ballet between the freedom of mind and the purpose of love's destiny in eternal fellowship, forever unbounded in a perfect communion of Spirit, Mind, and the perpetual physical made anew.

When we can get to a point of perspective where we no longer require this existence to define our value, we move closer to the Jesus Purpose. He is the conductor of creation and we gain the most wealth in this life by living in his grace each day, with each breath. This is the valued treasure that cannot be stolen, abandoned, or measured. But it can be invested.

This treasure is not meant to be hoarded like a Scrooge or be buried like a pirate. It's meant to be lavishly spent. It is a wealth whose amount is proportionally increased the more it is shared.

To give is to receive.

It's back to that same counterintuitive mindset not of this world; radical and unique. It would be of no value if there were nothing more to this single devoid blip of existence we call life. Yet throughout mankind's known measure of history, the concept has resonated.

Giving of self produces the treasure you will stockpile for eternity.

Chapter 9

The Clockmaker

THIS JESUS PURPOSE IS A CHALLENGING CONCEPT TO process. It is the idea of letting go of control. We are meant to give away our brokenness, pain, weakness, and fear to that which is unseen in order to allow light into the areas that we are ashamed to reveal. It feels invasive and our self-nature is to resist such intrusion.

We build emotional walls to protect our minds from such a personal invasion. These structures are a reactive measure to this broken world we experience daily; strongholds built from a history of wreckage from countless assaults of misplaced and broken trust. So much fear comes from this idea of an all-powerful God being invited into your uniquely fortified world. This life is overwhelming enough without the pressure of measuring up to a set of moral standards set by such an unconnected, outside entity.

In this bastion of self, draining moments turn into dragging days, which turn into periods of time that seem like an endless grind, a repetition of result and repair without reward, all until the walls are finally overcome and death invades. This is not what you were created to endure. You are not simply intended to survive on this life-filled, rotating cosmic ball stuck in a repetitive process of convenience, competition, and conquest.

Despite our walls of security, we still question the world outside and its offerings as it relates to our daily existence. Can the causer responsible for all that is really care about you? Does He even notice you hidden in the bunker you've created?

We've highlighted Jesus as the connection point which awakens desired relationship from your Creator. Despite what you may question, we're assured by him that this Creator God is concerned with the minuscule details of your life, that He is not mad at you and He wants what is best for you.

It's difficult to make reasonable connections between these trains of thought. These two perspectives appear that they cannot coexist reasonably. It becomes the great dichotomy of faith. Why and how would an omnipotent, omniscient Creator make all that is and then specifically match little ole you together within this specific place at this time? The sheer thought of such a God's greatness paired with our inadequate ability to simply question such greatness almost seems illogical.

In the world of religion, this is a well-debated and polarizing theological conversation. The thoughts and ideas become so taxing and combative that they have turned off countless people to the hope of such a life of purpose; a life of total freedom. How can a God who knows everything and who designed everything give someone true personal freedom?

In the world of theology this can form lines in the sand, like Predestination versus Free Will. Denominations and religious revolutions have been founded over this very type of question, each side drawing conclusions that could never be agreed upon by the countering perspective. These are the unsolvable mysteries of choosing to believe in the God of Jesus; an ultimate act of a faith in something greater. It mandates the question: Can you place your trust in that which is ultimately irreconcilable from our limited perspective?

You have either asked these type of questions yourself or turned a blind eye, afraid of the battle lines of demarcation and radioactive fallout. If you have asked these questions, you either fall into a divided camp of beliefs or you are left with me as an outsider, freed from conflict . . . the most amazing place to be.

If you have turned a blind eye, perhaps you will hear me out and find hope in a perspective that is somewhat unreasonable and illogical. If you fall onto one side of a divided line, you may be challenged. If you are seeking answers to help provide purpose and insight into the *why* of your life, then let me introduce to you the Clockmaker:

Imagine that all time and space, all matter and energy are held within the confines of a fixed structure—a giant clock. This clock was engineered with the most perfect precision ever developed. It began with a surge of initial energy from an unforeseen power, the Clockmaker.

Over a period of six days, the Clockmaker wound and rewound the clock, reintroducing momentum and power into its intricate inner workings. These inner workings are unique, more complex and dynamic than any human-created machine ever conceived. The clock's power is generated only by its Creator, but that energy is perfectly stored within veiled components of potential, a sustained source of complete energy that fuels the persistent kinetic mechanics which can easily be observed.

These inner workings, while designed with precision and fine-tuning, have a seemingly infinite quantity of random possibilities to trigger. Each trigger transfers its momentum into the next, a constant matrix of collisions and transference with no apparent measurable pattern.

This intricate design yields cause-and-effect outcomes which drive the predictable movements of the clock's hands. The hands move with perfect timing through the conclusion of each day, precisely maintaining both rhythm and direction in a constant and unchangeable manner. There are no right or wrong triggers. Each and every cause yields the same ultimate outcome, an effect, another choice of momentum which drives the continuation of movement to the clock's hands.

Now, the Clockmaker can choose to introduce His adjustments into the matrix array at any point and time He so chooses, but by design, the clock's product of precise calibration remains the same. Tick-tock.

On the seventh day, the Clockmaker rewinds the clock again with the same intended purpose. Another day begins. In this new day, the same cause-and-effect pattern remains. This time He has introduced a new factor . . . you.

You are now a part of the endless possibilities of this created mechanism of chaos with a precisely determined outcome. At a seemingly unaware moment in relative time you choose to order pizza over Chinese delivery—movement to the clock. You unconsciously awaken at 5:45 a.m. versus 6:02 a.m. . . . the clock continues to advance. You choose to continue to read this next sentence or put this book down altogether . . . tick-tock.

Nothing, absolutely nothing, escapes the inner workings of this clock.

The hands are set for a time, the end of the day. This is a final destination point and everything within the clock's mechanics will move forward until its inevitable conclusion comes. Free will and destination are both equal parts of its design. They drive the clock's very purpose and intent. There is nothing within the clock's engineering that can change what ***Will Be***.

It is an imperfect metaphor, but one which can provide helpful imagery to how what is irreconcilable to us can exist in a creation that is controlled from a greater force, a source of power that cannot be seen from within.

We're assured through Jesus that this is how God works with us. Before the foundations of the universe, there was a perfect plan created. You are a part of that plan. That plan, while from the perspective of outcome is perfect, the inner workings involve chaos and the unpredictable. This is observational. We are witnesses to it and participate in it at each and every moment.

Your Creator has the ability to adjust or intervene at any point in time, and He does so regularly, but His plan remains purposeful. It will come to a point when it stops, and there will be an end.

Now, while this might seem overwhelming or even inconsequential to you and your place within this fixed design, simply knowing the Creator's existence is real can stir emotions and raise questions. What is the nature of this Maker? Why would He allow such a seemingly unstructured environment?

Attempting to understand these irrational answers is the key. The Maker's desire is for you to simply realize He is responsible for everything. The Creator of everything desperately hopes that you can recognize through all the complexity, through all the chaos, through all the overwhelming uncertainty, that He is and He ***Will Be***, even after everything you know passes away.

Once you know His existence must be true, His desire is for you to seek His nature. For you to test, know, and fulfill the purpose of His plan.

This "clock" is only the beginning of His plans for you.

CHAPTER 10

The Exact Representation

BUCKET LISTS, EXERCISE, TREASURE, A GIANT OVERLY complicated clock, all are pointing you to a plan in which you were created to know. There is no testing which can deny it. There are thoughts, there are theories, there are alternatives, but there are no equals. The greatest intellectuals, philosophers, researchers, scientists, and more have dreamt of a day that can prove for or against the merit of its claims. There is not a created human who has not interfaced with it or heard its unspoken voice. By faith, you, personally, are called to proclaim or denounce it. To overcome or be overwhelmed through it. To accept or reject a simple invitation.

To know Jesus.

He is the exact representation of the Creator God. His character is a perfect and unbroken reflection of that which created and creates, an image you in your very essence bear.

The unified Spirit of that same entity has resided within the framework of creation since its foundations were laid, actively working through its structural mechanisms to move everything toward the ultimate conclusion of a plan that cannot be remotely fathomed from such a fixed focal point.

Today, Jesus is described through written words and eyewitness testimonies that only provide us with a taste of who he really is. These are the tangible and testable parts of him we can know, a literal part of human history, a physically material part of creation. The names he is given include, but are not limited to:

Love, Truth, Life, Light, Peace, Beginning, End, Bread, Water, Healer, Counselor, Almighty, Holy, Good, Blameless, Compassionate, Cleansing, Restoring, Teacher, Liberator, Victor, Anointed, Faithful, Revealer, Savior, Deliverer, Graceful, the Way, the Word.

This is the character, the conviction, and the promise of your Creator who longs to bring you inside the light of His revelation. The results and effects of this world alone are incomplete and unfulfilling, and freedom exists in that truth. The purpose of this creation and of your life is found in only one thing, the one thing you were created to need: to know Jesus.

I know at this point in this book, this is not a shocking conclusion. It seems too simple. Yet, at the exact same time, too complex. But, it is all that matters.

It is easier said than done to place all faith and all hope in a Jewish carpenter turned prophet. He did not exist to subject this world to condemnation, rather, he came to paint us a picture of what can be experienced beyond the limits of this life. He lived as a man to give us hope and a path to live on as we were truly intended, as eternal creations of freedom and light.

Jesus's life, death, and resurrection appear to be an unusual plan toward such an eternal process. We as creatures of thought, self-awareness, and creativity (in the image of our Creator) draw conclusions or ideas of how or why this is good or bad. Since the first human deliberate choice, mankind has chosen to focus on the details of processes, procedures, and thresholds—choosing to live in world of perceived responsibility where purpose is made through our own limited abilities. We've created the regulatory structure of this world and failed to find any course for hope beyond its universal boarders.

Jesus implored people to stop this cycle of self-created burden and heartache. He communicated that the laws of our nature were designed to lead us to him, to cast aside the thoughts of how you can better know God through your own efforts. He simply wanted us to observe his example and know that, without exception, the invitation of purpose in this life is found by placing hope in him.

That's it. Hope in Jesus.

Through that simple filter, this life here and now becomes an unabated outflow of love. It is the smallest taste of what ***Will Be*** that quenches the thirst for the purpose behind pain and suffering. This is where we glimpse to a period of fulfillment and past the present disappointment, emptiness, and futility. Everything changes now and forever when you choose to hope. Hope, faith, trust—synonyms of an active choice to believe. Committing to entrust, developing a personal confidence in what Jesus said and did.

From that point we are promised (guaranteed) to see change in our lives, in this creation. You are given a commitment from Jesus that the unified Spirit of your Creator will commune with your spirit in an unbreakable bond, providing a perspective that yields priceless and limitless resource. You have an endless and affixed access to all of the characteristics of Jesus:

Love, Truth, Life, Light, Peace, Beginning, End, Bread, Water, Healer, Counselor, Almighty, Holy, Good, Blameless, Compassionate, Cleansing, Restoring, Teacher, Liberator, Victor, Anointed, Faithful, Revealer, Savior, Deliverer, Graceful, the Way, the Word.

This is who your Creator God is and what He offers to you. He offers Himself. He is not angry with you. He wants what is best for you. He is pursuing you.

This is knowing Jesus.

CHAPTER 11

THE PROCESS OF MOVING

SINCE THE TIME THIS BOOK BEGAN TO TAKE FORM, MY family and I have relocated our home . . . twice. I now have a very strong opinion on the task of moving from one house to another. A process I am hopeful to avoid again for the vast foreseeable future. Simply put, moving sucks. Ask anyone who has moved, "Is it easy?" I can almost guarantee the answer.

That said, I have no doubt at all that we were right in line with our purpose as a family to go through the painful process of moving . . . twice.

My beautiful wife and I are rapidly approaching fifteen years of blissful marriage. Combine that with two preteen children, and you apparently accumulate a mass collection of *things*. These *things* can be looked at as either precious keepsakes or worthless junk, depending on the point of view. Every single item individually represents a portion of time, energy, and investment of some sort. Whether a fleeting moment or a large portion of a lifetime spent, all of these items have a story to tell.

Many of these *things* find their way out through a process of purging. We send away that which has lost its intrinsic value below the desired threshold of retaining. Those *things* that don't make the keep-cut are relegated to trash or recycle. They become relics of the past moved out to make room for the present or future.

The remaining *things* that do make the cut are packed and loaded to be relocated into a new setting. The same fixtures now find their abode in a new world. The purging process takes a new angle as some of the *things* kept in the hope of fitting in simply do not.

Nothing about this process changes the tangible connections we have to every object that exists. There is direct relationship to time and energy with everything, whether kept or purged; they are and always will be forever connected.

Marriage adds a unique element into this equation. In a healthy, thriving union, a couple releases the threats of invasion and willingly submits to a love free from traditional borders and walls, allowing all that they are and ***Will Be*** to be exposed and open to their partner. Every*thing* that is connected in time and energy to one is forever connected to both, and it forever becomes a shared investment.

We're given imagery and scripture indicating that the unified spirit of Jesus moves in, into your life. We're given the picture of marriage and union as the design of how this relationship should act and share. It is a process not of instantaneous result and reward, but rather an exploration in partnership.

You are offered the chance at a new perspective on what life is and how it should be lived. In union with your

Creator, as a being of creation, together you willingly submit to a love free from borders and walls. This is the purpose you were designed for. That relationship is easier written than done. Ask anyone who is married, "Is it easy?" and I can almost guarantee the answer.

Marriage is not about the result, it's all about the journey.

When we change our mindset of working toward God to working with God, our understanding of why we are called and why we exist changes. It is not about any result. It is about the experience! You are a being filled with connections to *things*, relationships to time and energy . . . and Jesus came to share in that journey with you to develop a lasting, eternal partnership of love, grace, and devotion.

In this process, the spirit of God moves within us and helps to move us into a new home.

The reason my wife and I had to move . . . twice . . . was that our second home—the intended destination—was being built anew. We literally contracted and invested in nothing, knowing what would be built for us. Through the process of construction, I collected some *things*, scraps of construction debris from the site as a reminder of what was being prepared. I kept those items on the dash of my truck to remind me daily that bigger and better things were ahead.

Jesus is a carpenter for a reason. He builds new *things*.

The Spirit of God is eager to get you packed and ready. To take all of the *things* you are connected to and put them in their rightful place. There are things that we feel need to be removed or purged, and those are taken care of. Your connections to those things can never be wholly broken, but they can be made part of a perfect plan of redemption.

Those things will always have connection to your story, but they no longer have to reside in the places you were created to dwell within. Those former spaces of pain, anger, and heartache are replaced with free, open space for present or future. This new home has been prepared for you, custom designed for your exact needs. This is the hope that a life built with Jesus offers. A new life that begins and transforms.

You are tested to move, you are not evicted from where you are by a set of regulations and restrictions that are forced. You are free to partner in this process because of the price Jesus paid. His life's purpose is made openly available to you because he freely chose to die for you. When we die to ourselves and our things and we accept the offer of his relationship in our complete worlds, we are liberated to begin the experience of eternity in this finite life. We are already destined for that, so anything now becomes part of the new adventure with Jesus alongside.

No one has ever said moving or marriage is easy . . . but when properly managed, rarely is the course of action not worth it. Where is your investment staked? Have you opened every door to your life and invited the Spirit of life inside to move you? Are you prepared to experience a peace and joy beyond any comprehensible rationale? What is holding you back from what is prepared just for you?

Remember, it is not about the result—it's about the journey.

CHAPTER 12

WHEN, NOT IF

READING OR WRITING OR THINKING OR RATIONALIZING are not actions of change. You have a part in the process. It is up to you to act.

As a dad, I have probably overused the phrase "talk is cheap." I desperately desire to instill in my children the knowledge that progress requires action, not merely contemplation.

This life of peace, hope, love, and joy is not sitting back to wait to see "if" hope and purpose happens. Seeking real life is a commitment to act, in faith, through the entirety of this existence. It is a moment-by-moment decision of choice not to quit on hope in Jesus, because at the end of it all, your Creator has hope for a forever-partnership with you.

I personally lived this most-valuable lesson in the confines of Paris Island Recruit Training Depot, where men and women are made into Marines.

Since a young age, I had always desired to commit a portion of my life in military service. The camaraderie, the honor, the courage, the uniformity, and the ideal of standing and fighting for freedom appealed to the core of who I am.

As soon as I was eligible, I raised my right hand and swore my allegiance before God to serve and defend the Constitution of the United States.

I was so eager to get the journey started that I did not even attend my own high school graduation ceremony, forgoing that secularly-viewed "special day" in pursuit of a greater promotion. For the next three months I would be reshaped, reconditioned, trained, and molded . . . made into something new, formed at the hands of instructors into a servant-warrior of destruction, purposed by winning and promoting earthly liberty.

This road of change was not easily traveled.

In order to reshape that which is already established, the old must be broken down to a state of malleability. The structure must be softened through a process of fire and relentless impact until the strength within yields completely and gives way to this necessary process of transformation. The brokenness endured to bring matter to this necessary state causes discomfort, pain, confusion, anxiety, and threat into every bond of what was and what ***Will Be***.

In the midst of this change, a point of complete submission is reached. Prior to this point, even while involved in the process, you consciously and subconsciously resist. But when you have nothing left and you completely relinquish your desire to even claim the title of worthiness, you are ready.

This is the point at which you become a Marine.

There is still a long road ahead, and you will not be called Marine for weeks more, but for the remainder of your training you are refined, polished, trained, molded, and strengthened into the warrior who stands ready to protect all that he has been blessed with. The process no longer becomes arduous, but rather engaging. You awaken, excited to see what new traits of strength or potential are revealed. You see the promise of joining the rank and file of honor, courage, and commitment, wearing a new and well-earned title of "The Few, The Proud."

This process was not walked alone. Weeks later, with nearly eighty brothers from platoon 2120, I graduated not across a high school stage, but across a drill field. I graduated my way.

The process was not without guidance and direction, rather it was a partnership of commitment with my four drill instructors, all of us equally desiring the foreseen outcome—an overcoming into something new, something we were all a part of, together.

It was not an "if" for them—it was a "when."

Despite my inability to see hope in the darkest of moments, when I believed it may not be possible, when I thought it may not be worth it, they were there to *help* me through. Now, often their offerings of "*help*" did not meet the expectation of assistance I would have personally chosen. It was often brutal, filled with discomfort, pain, confusion, anxiety, and threat. In the moment-by-moment walk of that experience, I learned to trust the process even though I was uncertain of the next day's outcome. I learned to become responsive in choice, not hesitating with "if" I should or could do what was ordered. It was in that transition that I learned to have faith and find a growing joy in who I was becoming; discovering strength and abilities far beyond my own realization.

Jesus never sees you as an "if."

When you know Jesus, when you place hope in Jesus, when you follow Jesus, you become part of a transformation journey greater than any warrior ever trained. You are part of a reformation process, and that process can be difficult in the midst of its fire and impact. It is a relentless emersion of grace, a process of learning unabated love in spite of the present broken and unwilling creation. It is an obstacle course that takes you from a strength of self to a strength beyond self—a test to overcome.

You do not walk this course alone. You are given a platoon of compatriots to help pick you up and dust you off. You are given instructors who laid the foundations of time and space, the unbounded champions of liberty who have seen the outcome, knowing there is not an "if" to foretell, but only a "when."

This pursuit of honor, courage, and commitment comes not by your limited abilities alone, but by the blood paid, which sealed an eternal contract and a covenant of partnership and promise to overcome this life's course together.

The road ahead will not be easy. You will be tested and trained. You own an active role in the process, moment-by-moment, choosing to be aware of the ongoing, unyielding love that is refining you. You may feel discomfort, pain, confusion, anxiety, and threat—these are signs of progress.

As you grow in this process, you will discover a new perspective. You will awaken engaged and begin to see the changes within. You will gain strength and capabilities not accessible before. With Jesus alongside, walking with you, helping you through that which is present and preparing you for what is ahead.

You will learn to trust the process despite uncertainty of the days to come. You will learn to have faith and find immeasurable joy in what you are becoming.

You begin to know, live, and thrive within the Jesus Purpose.

CHAPTER 13

KNOWING VS. UNDERSTANDING

TO KNOW PURPOSE IS TO TRUST PURPOSE. WE LIVE IN A culture and time where education is valued and elevated upon a pedestal as a pseudo-deity. The ever-accessible paths to schooling are boxed and packaged, marketed on billboards and infomercials, stamped, accredited, conformed, and regurgitated. Their ideals and principles provide a heartless array of finite insight and information without a shred of humility. They are bastions of the elite and self-proclaimed progressive.

Now, please do not misunderstand, education is important. Knowledge is powerful. Intellectual insight can provide clarity and awareness to almost anything tangible, but closed-environment knowledge will always have limitations.

Knowledge can never self-create, only imagination can. Imagination is an often disregarded character of human uniqueness. It is the ability for your living mind to concoct thoughts and realities that do not exist within the realms of testability. You have the means to create that which cannot ever be. You can give the figments of mind their own life, history, dimension, direction, and even purpose.

We can tangle our self-created perspectives around thoughts that can never be considered reality. A wholly constructed, individualized perversion of what is and what is to come. Human logic can create a fragile structure when assembling the building blocks of knowledge and imagination.

We imagine to develop an idea. That idea is then weighed against experience for validity. It is processed to be recognized, whether plausible or whimsy. There is no good or evil in this process. It is how we are designed. As our ideas are weighed against the reality we sense, they are stored and over time, ideas become ideals—a standard set of ingrained beliefs, a personal understanding of truth that cannot be easily removed. It is a self-created paradigm of reality in your mind. This filter of reality becomes your point of view.

These ideals begin at a point of life unknown to anyone. Through genetics, environmental exposures, and cultural influences, they shape our minds and make us who we are: uniquely unique beings.

Built on the foundations of creativity and knowledge, these ideals transition into an immeasurable, but very identifiable, characteristic—Common Sense. Your perceptions, your recognition, and your reactionary mindset are all formed from the sense of common structure you have built.

Also called wisdom, common sense is how you interact with the world. Wisdom is your reckoning of the ideals that have been created within yourself and the physical experience of interacting with the external universe you live in. They are the undeniable truths of your point of view.

Common sense built only with fixed-world knowledge is inherently flawed and wholly limited. Common sense built only with pure creativity is untethered and unreliable. These categories of common sense founded on self-manufactured ideals are therefore, by conception, myopic and imperfect.

So where does grounded, relevant, life-strengthening wisdom thrive?

Wisdom thrives in understanding.

Understanding is not an individual process—understanding involves more than a self-only comprehension. It assumes an agreement with another; a mutual trust of perspectives and relative truths.

There is a distinct difference in knowledge and understanding.

I know my wife. I know her likes and dislikes, strengths and weaknesses, hopes and fears. I have shared the most intimate earthly relationship possible with her for over fifteen years . . . but, I am regularly reminded, I do not fully understand my wife. As a man, I am convinced that it is an impossibility to fully understand her. I can never see and know things completely as she does.

When we take our knowledge, creativity, ideals, and wisdom and partner them into a resource greater than ourselves; a source who has revealed Himself as the author of existence and truth, we should realize that we can never fully understand Him.

This is where a personal relationship happens. It is at this point where a desire to understand drives a passion and an endless pursuit of communion. The Creator of all that is knows you . . . and just as He desires your communion with Him, He also longs to understand you.

Jesus spent time on earth not in constant religious study, not in the halls of the great intellectuals, not focused solely on beautiful song and art. Jesus spent his time with people, asking, inspiring, in fellowship, and in personal relationships—sharing in understanding.

Understanding is an amazingly freeing mindset to grasp hold of. The magnificence of understanding lies in the simple knowledge that you do not have access to all of the answers. It is a contradictory action of pursuit from what the intellectual champions of this world pontificate.

The nature of self-help, go-it-alone humanity is to seek out the black and white of the world, to know with certainty what is good or evil. It is to define everything into an acceptable group of fixed ideals and principles and sell those as a complete account of accredited truth.

This is the root of all religion.

A life focused on this practice—attaining knowledge for the purpose of defining ideals—is a dead-end road; a lifeless existence of comparison and hopelessness. Can you measure the uniqueness of a snowflake? No. Then how can we possibly believe we can find answers for everything? How do we find a balance between knowledge, imagination, and ideals?

This life is not about seeking knowledge for the sake of answers only. It is about a relentless demand for knowledge to draw an understanding of who you are and why you exist.

So you can find, know, hope, and trust in Jesus.

Through Jesus, you ***Will Be*** brought into a personal relationship of wisdom through God's spirit, and this will provide you with a peace in your life that passes all understanding.

Chapter 14

A World of Sin

SO HERE IT IS . . . THE DREADED THREE-LETTER WORD of religion, the dividing line between righteousness and you. The curse of humanity's struggle, the affliction of shame, the burden of unending correction and the torment of unescapable failure:

Sin.

If you're familiar with Christianity at all, you have a familiarity with sin. It is usually presented in one of two select blends (tailored for your religious preference). There's the "fire and brimstone; turn or burn" bold-roast, or the "we don't really need to talk about it because it makes people too uncomfortable" vanilla-flavored brew.

Neither were really Jesus's taste.

Jesus was real . . . Epically real. Jesus's life was so real and so epic, that his life left the most impactful, lasting effects on the course of humanity as a whole. Jesus did not mince words or wax poetic with directionless philosophy. He did not use fear as a tactic to coerce, nor did he shame people into a confession of compulsion.

Jesus was not afraid to talk about the state of mankind's hearts. He commonly spoke about how and why we were broken and used specific examples of life to elaborate on the complexities of creation—a creation designed for you to thrive within and overcome through. He took his message of hope and aimed it right into the bull's-eye of what we, in action, established as sin, and gave us the clearest path to overcoming its allure.

Sin has been the struggle of spirit-filled life from the earliest points of origin, and to this day it is the most misunderstood, misrepresented, and misguided "mechanism" that humanity fails to properly comprehend.

In any place where people commune, the powerful nature of sin consumes its prey as a venue of vultures, feasting on the lifeless corpses that have yielded to the worst strain of communicable disease that mankind has ever encountered. It is a virus that targets healthy relationships, against God and against one another.

Sin is an affliction, a widespread infection, responsible for all human death.

Through the course of mankind's history, we have been given rules, laws, and commandments; parameters set to guide us through this life. These safeguards of love were established to help us define what sin is and how we can identify its terminal effects.

Jesus took these rules of religion, the laws of safeguard, the commandments of humanity's requisite, and he summarized them in the simplest and most powerful of ways:

Love God with all that you are—Body, Mind, and Spirit
and equally as important,
Love one another as you love yourself.

With this simple but revolutionary summation, Jesus helped define who we were created to be and therefore established what we were also created not to be.

Jesus was making an extraordinary point when he directed that sin is anything that is not based in love—toward God or toward one another. Sin is a condition that we cannot escape, we cannot avoid, we cannot evade. No one has ever measured up to the standard that Jesus set. It is impossible—it is how you were born:

Free to choose to love, compelled to choose law.

The collective, universal Church understands this divide well. We recognize that all mankind has fallen short of the love we were created within. Religion, throughout its reign, has pointed us to the need for a change. It has championed a mission of reconciliation through salvation. A saving of yourself (with God's help) based on your action or actions of repentance.

This idea of repentance is directly tied to the words of Jesus and his apostles. It has become a calling card of the evangelical, episcopal, catholic church. It is an identifying trait of those aligned behind the righteous and just, the omnipotent God of wrath and power. Repentance became a way of showing others how you publically honor God and prove how much you love Him through steadfast obedience.

We show devotion to God by reflecting this in how we control our behavior and leave our old lives of sin behind us in the dust. We go and sin no more (or, we at least do our best and hope no one notices).

This has become common church philosophy. A pattern of self-control shows and proves to the world that you follow God. Through this process of repetitive confession and pious conduct, you are then contracted with the responsibility to share this testimony through the means of judgment and conviction. You are now obliged to educate others in their necessary removal of immoral behavior and encourage them to follow in this programmed process of obedient submission. You are entrusted to become a pledged warrior of allegiance in this daily battle against sin in yourself and in others.

In this religious culture, you are given authority to provide council and discernment in the rights and wrongs of society. You now are an advocate for God's way. You are christened and compelled to convert others by helping them learn how to control the way they act, holding them accountable to their arduous walk of "repentance." You are a part of the collective fellowship, appointed to ensure behavior is always "good." This is the outward signal that your salvation is real and you are acceptable to a governing God.

The only problem with this idea of repentance . . . It is dead wrong.

You see, the problem with the Church, not unlike the problem with the world is this: It is full of people. It is full of the sinners, the screw-ups, and the desperate—all trying to figure this life thing out.

Sin is inescapable, unavoidable. It is not who you are, but *where* you are. Sin is unloving and unhealthy, and it cannot be completely escaped in this creation. We, people, interpret repentance, and we, people, redefine its process. We, people, have created a system that allows judgment and condemnation to be the primary identifiers of the Church. That is an effect of *religion*.

Religion bears many titles, many labels. Religion is not limited to a theistic process, despite what the atheistic preach. Religion is a manufactured product created, established, defined, reformed—etc. etc., ad infinitum—by humanity. Religion exists because our self-aware nature chose to seek knowledge in who we are and what life is all about. However, religion will never provide any substantial answer to the whys of our life's purpose.

As perplexing as it may seem, you were created to rebel, to question your place and purpose. You were fashioned to test and learn. You are not called to understand other people's definition of your living world. You are made to find hope and purpose in your world. You were made to seek out, experience, and attempt to draw understanding from Jesus's unusual perspective: Love God, love one another.

So then, just what did Jesus mean when he told us to repent?

The word 'repentance' in Greek literally translates to "to change your mind." Despite what you have been told or what you experienced, repentance has no relational correlation to the actions of sin. Repentance is an action of personal choice, not out of obligation or coercion, but out of recognition.

Repentance is a mental exercise, a continuous and repetitive process of acknowledging and drawing understanding of God's truth. It is a personal, internal reminder to meditate on grace and love. It is the refocusing of your mind, your spirit, and your actions toward a perspective of love, demonstrated perfectly by the life of Jesus.

Sin is real and it manifests in more ways than are often realized. The spiritual world is confusing and complex. We see its effects, its broken, perverted manifestations, and we feel a compelling of self to call it out. We feel we can help correct and change these actions of "sin" toward an outcome that is better. We brandish our weapons of criticism and judgment in our desperate attempts to "help" God. We try to assist Him in redirecting and combatting the sins of this world. It's a worthy attempt, but it is a worthy attempt from the unworthy.

Jesus is clear: We are all broken. We all have sinned. You were not created to change others; you were created to LOVE others.

Comparing any sin against another sin takes us right back into the spiraling process of falling away from the wonder of grace. It was in the first actions of mankind's free rebellion, where we desired to know right and wrong, good and evil. The initial action which led to original sin was not the consumption of the fraudulent fruit. It was in the redirecting focus away from the tree which provided them all that they would ever need: perfect sustenance, The Tree of Life.

But abandoning perfect sustenance did not exclude us from perfect love.

Perfect love gives us the freedom to have that choice. A choice of a life lived in law or a life lived in love. This perfect love offers us the freedom to know a life apart from the Creator God. In our collective, intellectual, physical, and spiritual rebellion—in a moment of redirection and faith forgone—we untrusted the truth of God's perfect endowment. This perfect freedom, this perfect love's plan, became the disease of sin.

Sin did not make humanity bad; it gave them awareness. It opened their eyes and minds to the doors of what love is not. But law took the place of love, and in that moment, control replaced love.

Humanity chose perpetual control, a desire to control self and a yearning to control others. Sin is, in all ways, the opposite of freedom. It is the antithesis of love. Sin is oppressive, enslaving, addicting—sin takes control of your eternal destination. Sin is not what we do, it is not who we are. Sin is *where* we are.

It is not a physical place, but rather is it is a state of being. As with so much of this wonderful adventure called life, this freedom of control is a paradox beyond our ability to fully understand. Control is made in our choices. Having choice is having freedom. Freedom is love. Choosing anything other than love is sin . . . Life and freedom are found in releasing our sense of control. We release ourselves needing to have control by changing our minds to focus on Love.

Got that?

Not really? Me neither.

It is beautifully complex and remarkably simple. There are no actions that can attain its ultimate reward. It is only through faith—the final yielding of trust into this plan of perfect sustenance, Jesus—where hope finds its purpose in your world.

You were not created to be in control of this life. You were not created to change yourself or to change one another.

You were created to love and be loved.

Sin, regardless of how it manifests, happens whenever we lose focus of that.

Real, peaceful, life-producing personal change is not a reflection of self-repentance or confession, nor in believing you have any measure of control in your own eternal salvation. Rather, your change is a reflection of perfect freedom's spirit, a living love inside of you, making you more complete, being prepared for an everlasting journey with Jesus. Slowly, from deep within, you become transformed, no longer subjected to this world's demands for comparison, criticism, judgment—oppression, enslavement, addiction. You come to realize that you are completely loved and you are awakened to the truth that you are viewed as completely sinless in the eyes of your Creator!

Yes! From God's perspective you are not infected with the disease of sin at all! There is nothing that can break that truth. Sin is dead—left in an empty tomb—conquered completely. A perfect plan of total freedom wholly reconciled, sin only has power should it be given power to maintain control over you.

You alone cannot outmatch the desire to control . . . Remember, you require help. Sin only has power when you choose to go it alone. Its overwhelming appeal and allure, its ever-present lie, its lust of control is that you alone can outmatch grace.

You will wage battle in this war for the remainder of this life moment-by-moment, conflicted between the perspectives of control and love. The cure—the only hope we have—is Jesus.

So repent! Change your mind. Refocus on the grace of an unbounded Creator.

There is a plan that extends far beyond the ability to rationalize. Learn to trust in love . . . Repent!

Find, know, hope, trust, understand, and focus on Jesus.

Jesus is sufficient, and his love is all that you need.

Chapter 15

A Plan of Action

This journey with Jesus is unlike most of our routine social interactions. It is not a grind of apathetic, repetitive, mindless learned behaviors. It is also not a whirlwind of pure bliss. It is a partnership.

As a leader in our small business, I have had a recent change of perspective on the word "relationship." "Relationship" is descriptive of a connection without any indication as to the nature of that connection. Anything you have connected with, in any way, you have a relationship with. In our ever-evolving plan to make our business better, we have recently been undertaking the process of rebranding. Our business has been well established for over ten years, and we needed to communicate to our market how we've grown through that process.

We are no longer the same firm we were when we began. I wasn't even an employee when it began. With specialized consultation, we are attempting to take who we are becoming and meld it with who we started as, all while keeping the foundational core of what we know ourselves to be.

It's a long and thought-provoking process, reflecting and refining a message of who we ***Will Be***.

Relationship was one of the centric words used throughout our company's historic brand messaging, provided as a descriptor of who we are and how we work with our clients . . . *"We are relationship-focused."*

However, through the process of this re-messaging, rebranding, and fine-tuning our identity, I recognized the lack of power the word "relationship" holds and how it truly falls flat. In the context of who we are with our most valued clients, "relationship" means almost nothing. Just because we have a relationship with our clients, it does not inherently make our interactions with them good or beneficial. It simply means they know of us and have had some generic form of interaction with us. We needed to stop using this undescriptive, lifeless word.

The truth is, we were not a "relationship company." By simple definition, "company" indicates an existing or established relationship. *Every* "company" is a relationship entity—that is the meaning of that darn word!

I knew we needed to change what had become an embedded part of our internal vocabulary. We need to replace "relationship" with a word that did communicate who we were and who we were committed to continue being . . . I suggested we refocus our energy onto "partnership."

"Partnership" is so much more than a mere relationship. The relationship is assumed, and now the word gains the power of being mutually beneficial.

That is who we were, who we are, and who we are committed to be. "Partnership" describes exactly who we want to be known as. We were not a "relationship-focused company"—we are a "partnership-focused company." We exist to support our clients and develop lasting engagements of support, value, commitment, excellence, and growth. When they win, we win.

This small shift in a single word changes the communication of who we are more so than any other single word.

For as long as I can remember, I have heard how our God is relationship-focused. He wants a relationship with you. Now I ask you, what the junk does that mean?

If an omnipotent Creator exists, and we've established a process for surveying that, It would by common definition have a relationship with us, even a personal relationship. It could have a desire to be close to us as individuals or not. The word "relationship" means nothing when describing the nature of the two companies' interactions with one another.

You were born into relationship with your Creator. You have no choice in that matter. You can choose to deny it, avoid it, or embrace it, but the relationship is fixed. It was established at the beginning of time and set upon a course toward a destination beyond what a human mind can imagine.

So our God is, in His nature, a Relationship-God, and everything that exists is in relationship with Him. It is how God was, is, and forever ***Will Be***. But, your Creator is so much more than a Relationship-God. He is a God of partnership!

From our Creator's very first personal revelations to mankind, God described Himself as "We." "We," as in collective. "We," as in being in permanent company with one another. The three-in-one Creator "We": the triune, Father-Son-Spirit. "We" being a universal partnership of support, value, commitment, excellence, and growth; the perfect reflection of how you are designed and what you are made to thrive within—Partnership.

Jesus came to save the world from the idea that we are in relationship with God. Jesus came to rebrand from the established idea that there is some manner in which you and I can produce the means to elevate into His grace. Jesus did not change who God is, but he came to tell us who God forever ***Will Be***—a God of perfect partnership, and He has invited you into His Company.

Now, you are probably thinking if this is a partnership, then you must therefore give into this company equally in order to make it mutually beneficial. But how can you possibly give God something He benefits from? Herein lies the path which must be taken for the Jesus Purpose journey ahead. Seeking not what you must give to God, but learning what God most desperately desires from you: who you were made to be.

You.

The Creator created your individuality, your unduplicatable uniqueness, your personal, living triune reflection of His image, to simply be united completely with the "We"—God.

Jesus came to save the world—not to condemn it. Jesus rebranded the misplaced perspectives of humanity's ideas of God. He took what was undescriptive and lifeless, and gave it a personal, indefinable identity. He became man. Jesus partnered in this creation as a living, breathing, flesh-and-blood person. A walking, talking partner in this process with you.

It became all about this change of focus to partnership from this point forward—an action—a change of mind.

Know with confidence that you were designed to bask in the mutually beneficial, intimate relationship of grace, and be open to freely give all of who you are to your Creator. Then, inside this partnership of love, you are made prepared to offer that same unabated partnership to other people.

CHAPTER 16

WALK THE WALK—TALK THE TALK

MY FAMILY AND I ARE BLESSED TO BE A PART OF AN AMAZing church in Woodstock, Georgia. Our church mission is to "Love people to Jesus." It's a special place, and I am honored to be a part of such an eclectic, loving, and transparent group of real people. It's unlike any other church I have experienced.

This is not cliché. It is not a criticism of other individual churches. It is just my observation.

Individual churches are not unlike you and me. They are each unique and serve a bigger purpose to our collective partnership with God. The study of the Church is a fascinating look into history, theology, science, and physiology. From the last words of a resurrected Jesus, a mission has been set forth to share the "good news," and from the time of those last words of a resurrected Jesus, there have been human differences in how that mission should be accomplished.

The collective Christian Church has been the most transformative force in the history of mankind; conquering empires, establishing kingdoms, championing ethics and law, offering hope and unity, and setting an unparalleled ideal of earthly human freedom. The Church, despite what is commonly thought or taught, is more responsible for the improved quality of life throughout the self-aware world. This is testable and provable.

But, it is not without its share of bumps along the way. Despite what often is anticipated or desired, the Church is far from perfect.

And that's okay.

We were created in relationship. We do not get to choose our role or place; we do not get to define the considerations. You exist in relationship to the universe, the earth, to life, to humanity, to your family, to yourself—Body, Mind, and Spirit.

We thrive in partnership with our Creator, with Jesus, in a marriage, with our careers, with our teammates, with ourselves—Body, Mind, Spirit—and in the Church.

Once we come to know Jesus as our purpose, we are connected not by choice, but by love and grace to the rest of humanity. We are to love one another as we love ourselves. In partnership with Jesus, we are combined in unified purpose with others who have found hope and peace in this unusual Jewish prophet.

The Church isn't a building, it isn't a denomination, and it is not a group of rule followers or rule makers. The Church does not exist to control or enslave, judge or condemn, excommunicate or summon. The Church exists to love!

We are partners in the adventure of grace, called on to love one another as we have been loved by our Creator.

We gather to celebrate our newfound hope in life, to give expressions of gratitude to a living God of mercy and purpose. We share our experiences in this journey and help each other draw closer to understanding that which is beyond our ability to understand, growing in wisdom and hope.

Together we are united in this corporation of purpose, collectively called to share with others this message of perfect love and underserved grace. This is the "good news" that Jesus instructed us to deliver.

The closer we are to this purpose of drawing nearer to Jesus, the healthier the Church will be. It's also likely that as a Church becomes more like Jesus, the more persecuted they will become—by law, by religion, by the world. This message of "good news," while life changing, is not for the shy or timid. It is a message of action and sacrifice, fixated on a time and place that ***Will Be***.

Jesus perfectly understood, lived, and loved in this way. He provided us an example to follow, words to investigate, and a promise of eternity to meditate upon. His message is challenging and direct, and it gives us insight into how we are to interact with the world. You were created not to be conformed into this broken world's point of view. With Christ we are transformed, given insight from the "We's" perspective.

However, you are also not intended to have a point of view that ignores or condemns this world. The cultural church is not the same as the Church that is the Body and Bride of Christ. It is important to develop awareness and perspective on the distinct differences. The two concepts of the church will challenge and cause conflict among your own part of this partnered congregation. It becomes, as a collective, the same struggle we face as individuals.

Together, we jointly engage in the struggle of purpose and process. We exist to love, but the execution of love is so much more complex than can be described in reasonable context. What we end up with is a process that leads to controlling, judgment, condemnation, used-car sales tactics, and petty competition.

This is how much of the world sees the church. It is the cultural appearance of Christianity. It is seen as a den of robbers and liars, hypocrites and blinded theologians, as a group of humanity focused on spreading its news through fast-hitting, impersonal evangelism and guilt-conjuring messages of penitence. This church exists, and it is powerful. But this is not the Church that is changing the world through love.

The Jesus-partnered, love Church exists too. It is awake, aware, and more powerful than the cultural church could ever imagine.

The Church united in grace and love that accepts anyone and everyone, casts out fears, and offers hope and help is found within the same walls of every cultural church. It is yet another paradox that we need to be ever-mindful of. As people connect to one another through the Creator's Spirit and are called into purpose through Jesus, we are not put in place to be the monitors of the present. We are called to be ambassadors of an endless future.

In our limitations, our self-defined isolated point of view, we can become trapped in the narrow-focus of the here and now. The message of hope through Jesus is not about a better now. It is about a perfect forever.

The concept of eternity is often used in ill-fitting or limiting context. If eternity is true, it offers *everything*!

There is nothing outside of the boundaries of this life that cannot be remedied.

This is the message of the living Church of Jesus; to extend its hands to anyone and offer a beacon of hope and purpose to this gift of life. You, as part of this Church, are a messenger of freedom and grace to all who are open to the idea of more than random happenstance.

We are born with a desire to challenge, yet we crave for a hope beyond the grave. We are limited by only ourselves and our collective point of focus, and it is a unique trait that you as a spirit-connected person possess to ignite the potential ability which will cause immeasurable impact to the entire living world.

This is the real Church. This is your part in the Church: There ***Will Be*** only one Judge and there ***Will Be*** only one path to acquaintance. There is nothing anyone can do to earn it. It can only be accepted for the gift of grace that it is. That Judge is not me. That Judge is not you. That Judge is not us.

The Church is created to love. It is intended to love and offer unlimited grace with an eternal perspective. When the Church, like the individual, focuses the perspectives of purpose with partnership, connected intimately with Jesus, it loses its desires to focus on politics, law, judgment, condemnation, idols, and attendance. Instead, it becomes a living reflection of Jesus and his love for the world.

The real Church is the hands and feet of an alive Jesus, a perfect partner that no man can divide, a beacon of forever-freedom and the champion of hope that cannot be measured or fully understood.

The real Church is the embodiment of overwhelming love and the execution of amazing grace.

CHAPTER 17

FIGHTING THE GOOD FIGHT

AS I HAVE MENTIONED, I AM A COMPETITIVE PERSON. A very competitive person . . . I'm probably more competitive than you.

I have a younger sister, two years and two months younger, and to this day we constantly are in some level of subconscious competition. It is a battle that has produced both positive and negative history. We are very, very different people. I am analytical at heart—I process, test, deduct, act, adjust, and press forward toward set and focused objectives. When obstacles present themselves, I adapt, improvise, and overcome. My sister is the consummate artist, a dreamer who sees the colors and profiles of the embraced moment. She's able to react as life happens, adjusting midstream to how the brushstrokes fall onto her canvas of life. She has an idea of what it may become, but gets there in a very free-flowing manner.

Despite our differences, we share two alike and powerful characteristics: competitiveness and Jesus.

Aside from the obvious genetics, that's about where we separate as individuals.

Our relationship has had its collective share of ups and downs. We do honestly love each other, even when it's not easy. It's been a battle for years to see eye-to-eye on many things. That all said, when united together we are a force to be reckoned with. My wife learned this firsthand in a "harmless" family game of Monopoly. When on the same team, with the same desired outcome, my sister and I are an unstoppable force of destructive victory and unconscious resolve. We will not lose, even if we have to cheat to win.

Without a single word spoken, we harmoniously understand each other's driven nature . . . nothing but total domination ***Will Be*** the only acceptable outcome. To this day we are not allowed to be partnered when we're playing a game with my family. The usual excuse is "because they cheat," but my sister and I know it's really because when we're united, we're nearly unbeatable.

The idea of a perfectly harmonious partnership is laughable when we think about it in the context of the experienced world. So why do we think it should be this way with God?

There's an unspoken perspective and culture that God wants obedience and subordination as the primary mechanisms of our relationship with Him. This could not be further from the truth. In recorded interpersonal relationships found throughout the Bible and written history, we will find that challenge and fighting are much more common than obedience and submission. From Adam to you, we have all lived in a battlefield, a war waged to find freedom for ourselves and control over others—including from our Creator.

Men and women in scripture are found challenging the purpose set in front of them, struggling to align themselves with the unknown outcomes of benefit and blessing they're certain to produce. Conflict is a pattern of behavior that is pervasive and proliferative throughout the written records of prophetic history. The very expansions of all time and space, from the cosmos to the known aspects of all life, appear to be waged in this ever-present exercise of struggle.

It is in the midst of this fighting where truth becomes revelation. Conflict, despite its destructive by-product, reveals a supernatural freedom. Albert Einstein once wrote that "God doesn't play dice with the universe." Dr. Gerald Schroeder, an MIT trained physicist and Orthodox Jewish theologian, expanded on Einstein's quote by writing, "Einstein was correct. God does not play dice with the universe, but God allows the universe to play dice."[1] For as far as we can scientifically measure and calculate, the universe, despite the unfathomable order that undeniably exists, has an equal component of chaos and unpredictability. This natural freedom, just as undeniable, also exists.

Natural freedom, when viewed through a lens of the Judeo-Christian faith, interprets directly to a gift of love. Everything, therefore, is created in love.

---

[1] Gerald L. Schroeder, *God According to God: A Physicist Proves We've Been Wrong about God All Along*, 102.

As a man, Jesus was the physical manifestation of love, a literal, testable component of this creation. Through Jesus, we are shown that love's perfect process is not waged through the power of law and control, but rather through grace and selflessness. This is the eternal hope of what our struggle to know truth is all about.

Just like with my sister, when we are partnered with Jesus, with God, with the Holy Spirit we are not indebted under the power of judgment, but united with a purpose of victory at all cost. Together, we are an unstoppable, unbeatable team.

Despite the history you may have with God, your inevitable outcome is established. Victory has already been guaranteed, so the challenges of tomorrow bring a new perspective of peace and assuredness. You can begin the process now, aligning yourself with Jesus's goals of love, grace, and selflessness. The chaos and unpredictability of tomorrow will no longer be a domain for fear and uncertainty, but a refuge for hope and gratitude.

This is the good fight.

CHAPTER 18

THE ROAD AHEAD

I AM SITTING OUTDOORS AT A SMALL COFFEE HOUSE IN Carlsbad, California, just off the Coastal Highway, the ocean not far away. I have traveled to southern LA for work, planning to combine a business trip with short a family visit.

I have an uncle who lives in San Diego, and whenever I'm this close it only makes sense to travel the short distance and spend valuable time catching up. I wrapped up work early for the day and headed down I-5. Making better time than I had predicted and not wanting to be too early, I decided to make a stop and enjoy an unplanned moment of opportunity; to write, to ponder, to be grateful, and to simply be still.

In the Carlsbad Coffee House, there overwhelms a fragrant aroma of fresh roasted coffee. A young man, obviously a surfer, sits nearby, reading from Second Corinthians. It's a near-perfect moment in an imperfect place. I sip my extra dark-roast blend and think about where this book leads next. If you're still reading, which you must be, you have traveled my wandering stream of thoughts to this point, all collecting in an array of ideas, challenges, and resolutions.

Again, this is not a book on theology. It is a book about a journey. A road that we all take, a road of really living this one chance at life.

At times we find ourselves speeding down the interstate, almost unaware of our surroundings, with our minds engaged in the moments of past or future. This is where we spend an amazing amount of our lives: trapped in that which has already come and gone or that which may never happen.

It's normal. It's not a problem in its essence, but, like anything else, it can become a problem when it becomes the constant, overwhelming driving force of our life . . . an addiction of constrained perspective, trapped in that which is not presently accessible.

As you now know, I believe our lives are meant for a purpose. Every moment drives you with and toward greater opportunity, an unending process of growth. It is the choice you must make. You are either part of a creation or a fortunate, hopeless accident. If you acknowledge that you are created, then you must also realize you have purpose. That purpose thrives in the now.

Up to this point, we have looked into the whos, whys, and hows of God, Jesus, others, and your part in it all. For the remainder of this book, we will focus on two remaining key components of the Jesus Purpose:

- The Practical Application of the Jesus Purpose
- The Final Answer: ***Will Be***

Our personal journeys should be filled with way more Carlsbad Coffee Houses and much fewer zombie-like interstate hauls. The interstate serves a wonderful purpose, do not misunderstand the metaphor. When traveled effectively, it can allow us to expand our horizons well beyond the point of what we'd be capable of otherwise. It is the conduit to knowledge, power, reach, interaction, reconciliation, and wisdom . . . but the joy of fulfillment will not be experienced on those nonstop paths.

Together, we will look into how and when to deviate our life's routes, balancing the expanses ahead with the stops of enrichment along the way. These hidden coastal highways, boulevards, and avenues are where life's forever-treasures are stockpiled, grown, and matured. The off-path adventures are where exercise finds its value, where time becomes now, where your Creator's Spirit speaks to you, where rest is real and true peace is found.

Perspective becomes ***relevant*** in these places.

The word origin of "relevant" means "to raise up." It is time to raise up a new awareness of our personal worlds; to open our eyes, minds, and hearts to a struggling culture desperate for the "good news," all yearning for a real life of fulfillment, joy, and hope.

It is time for Jesus to be relevant.

Chapter 19

The Tools of Application

In the past few years I have become quite the handy guy. I have learned a newfound appreciation for craftsmanship and creativity. In the process of multiple moves, a new house, and my wife's various furniture restoration projects, I have had to learn many of these skills by immersive application, you know . . . trial by fire.

Recently I undertook a daunting project. Above the landing of our staircase in our new home is a large, blank wall which needed an equally scaled impact piece to fill the void and add much needed character. I decided to take my novice handyman skills and apply them toward a very large piece of active art. With no conscious thought as to providing an associated parallel to earlier chapters, my intention was to create a giant clock.

Kristina and I had been eyeballing a very large, abandoned, wooden wire spool in our under-construction neighborhood. This lightly damaged contraption had been aging beautifully in the Georgia sun, red clay, and periodic drenching thunderstorms. Its circumference on the flat end pieces measured a little over four feet, the ideal size for the time-keeping experiment I envisioned.

One Sunday after church, we mustered up the courage to walk across the undeveloped lot in our neighborhood, take possession of this seemingly worthless scrap of rejected waste, and get to work. We rolled it down the street and into our yard. When I got it onto our back patio and attempted to disassemble the large, round end piece that had I intended to use for the clock face, I discovered that the steel hardware securing the gigantic spool together was completely rusted and locked in place. After several attempts to loosen and break the large threaded bolts from the square nuts, I yielded to the fact that these metal rods would need to be cut.

I first unsuccessfully attempted to slice them manually with a hacksaw. The awkward positioning and the small working area made this task unusually complicated and difficult. I gave up defeated . . . temporarily.

I knew what I needed to get the job done, but there was a problem. I did not have what I needed to get the job done. This unique task required a specific tool, something which could effectively and efficiently cut through the rods in this specific situation. I needed a Sawzall.

If you are unfamiliar with a Sawzall, also called a reciprocating saw, it's basically the greatest tool on earth. It looks like a futuristic machine gun, complete with trigger and handle, and on its front end is an exchangeable saw blade which, when activated, moves back and forth rapidly, doing the arduous work of slicing destruction with joyful ease.

A few days later, while walking through the aisles at Home Depot, I convinced my beautiful bride that I needed this perfectly designed tool to complete my promised timekeeping decorative project. With a little convincing and hope-filled eagerness, she agreed to let me buy it! It was a great day in personal history. I was now the proud owner of a fluorescent green, eighteen volt, cordless Sawzall, the most versatile and manly of all power tools. Within minutes of being home, without complication or fanfare, the task was complete.

After assembly of the delicate mechanics, numeral painting, varnishing, and the addition of hanging hardware, the clock was finished and showcased, providing a useful and memorable story of adventure. This clock is a representative image of our arrival into a renewed life in our brand-new home. All it took was desire, recycled imagination, some humility, hard work, and the right tool for the job.

When I have a power tool in my hands, especially one like the awesome Sawzall, I find it entertaining to imagine what Jesus, the anciently trained carpenter, would think. I can almost see his eyes widen with awe and enthusiasm over something so cool, so powerful, and so multi purposed.

Tools are not only purposeful, but when they are appreciated in their uniquely applicable role, they're fun and remarkably valuable. The key to a great tool is its specific and distinctive capacity to perform an exclusive task in a project. Like the Sawzall, some tools are multifaceted, while others have very defined and limited jobs. That said, the value of any specific tool is not judged by either of these factors. A tool's value is wholly dependent on its craftsman's ultimate purpose. What does he need to get the job done? There is nothing better than the exact tool for the specific task at hand.

Guess what? You are a tool.

Sorry to outright call you such a term, but you are. You are a tool. You have a specific role for your craftsman. You have a specific, unique purpose with Jesus. You are the most valuable resource for his impact in this world. In the mindset of applying the tools for this Jesus Purpose, in this one-chance life, we must understand the traits we are equipped with.

What are the specific characteristics which help you have the greatest personal contribution of impact for the Jesus Purpose in this world? Every spirit-filled person has these resources and characteristics available within them. They are the key traits to being an effective and efficient means of impact, an instrument of precision who works closely with Jesus, focused in the ongoing work of love for our Creator God.

I have identified five traits which are the key components that refine and sharpen us to be used often and with immeasurable significance for an eternal outcome. These traits produce an awareness that allow us to travel far off course from the mainstream and display the confidence of the supernatural during our quest.

These traits equip you to become who you are intended to become. They are who, with Jesus, you ***Will Be***.

The next five chapters will focus individually on each of these key traits:

- Engagement
- Participation
- Selflessness
- Gratitude
- Hope

These traits are all available in your personal toolbox. Now it is time to put them to work.

Chapter 20

Trait 1—Engagement

WHENEVER I HEAR THE WORD ENGAGEMENT, I AUTOmatically think of the process of getting married. In a relationship of love, two people commit themselves to one another, pledging to become bonded partners for life.

It's an interesting tradition when you think about it. An engagement is promising to promise, committing to commit. It's a public expression of two agreeing parties being betrothed into a lifelong covenant.

Engagement is an active awareness of love's purpose in the life ahead and a period of time to plan for the complete unionization of two fully invested individuals who plan to legally, physically, and spiritually become connected as one.

My beautiful bride and my engagement story is a fantastic account we love to share. After dating for only two weeks, I knew that she was someone I was excited to share all of my life with. Smart, funny, kind, sexy . . . In those very early developmental days of relationship, I chose this breathtaking young woman who I barely understood, and I chose to love her—all of her.

Over the course of the next several weeks, we shared ideas of life and enjoyed each other's personal company, and became increasingly physically bonded through playful sessions of full-on making out. It was an exciting romance of passion, and we were both fully vested in each second of each moment we spent together. The simple presence of togetherness made everything complete. It was time spent soaking in the present.

After only two months of dating and a whirlwind of learning and yearning, I began my planning with permission from her dad. I called ahead to an intimate jazz bar in Atlanta named Café 290, making key arrangements for the forthcoming evening. I picked up Kristina and she had no clue what lay ahead. I had been blessed to inherit a ring that I never could have afforded; it had belonged to my great-grandmother. I had it, my guitar, emboldened courage, and a nearly bulletproof plan.

Dinner was fantastic, the accompanying music set the perfect mood. I told Kristina that I had accidentally left my wallet in my always pimpin', late '90s, silver Hyundai Elantra four-door. Little to her knowledge, this was all part of a well-concocted scheme. In advance, I had arranged to sneak back into the restaurant through the kitchen and appear on stage as the band took their break.

The set ran unexpectedly long—disturbingly long.

I knew that Kristina had to be freaking out, and boy was she. Thoughts of panic were running though her mind. "Where is Bill? Has he been mugged? Did he abandon me? WHAT COULD POSSIBLY BE GOING ON?!"

And then, truth was revealed. I had never left. Instead a scared-to-death, terrible guitar-playing, skinny white-boy was going to humiliate himself in front of a racially diverse crowd who came to enjoy their evening with cool drinks and cooler tunes.

The moments of singing and playing escape me. There were hindsight comparisons made to "Goat-boy" from Saturday Night Live of the '90s, but it didn't matter to me. She was my focus, she was my purpose in those lived-in-present moments . . . I wanted to let everyone know that I wanted to be with her, this woman, for as long as I lived this life.

The song I attempted to sing I had written just for her weeks prior. On a night we had planned to be together, she was keeping me delayed from seeing her. She was preparing a romantic picnic for two in her apartment. I was so desperate to be with her; longing to just be in her presence. But she was making me wait!

So during this painful process of gut wrenching apprehension and desire, I wrote a song. Its title: "Just Wait." Its chorus: "Just wait and see what's in store for us." These are the words that I offered to her just before I asked her to promise to promise, commit to commit.

That night, after I had gone all in and put myself out there, she did not say "yes." Thankfully, she did not say "no" either. She silently accepted my offer in timid excitement.

The crowd erupted with shouts of joy, applause of celebration, and words of blessing. She was stunned, knocked completely from her place of panic to a state of wonder and fear. She had no clue how this happened. She had no clue her parents already knew. In fact, she waited a couple of days before calling them to share the news, worried as to what they might think.

We officially married in April of 2000, before friends and family and became imperfect people, partaking in a perfect partnership, fully united in the promise of a promise, the commitment of a commitment.

Engagement in life is a daily choice to promise ourselves to live love. Engagement is a state of active awareness, a chosen mindset that this life is more than existence, and that our part in the world is meant to be connecting to it in the present. It is a mindful decision to pull your head from the proverbial sand in the ground and take part in the growth of relationship, with Jesus and with other people.

You were created in the state of relationship, but you must choose to engage with it. It is a promising to promise, a commitment to commit, a process to become lost in the desires and longing for love's impact in every part of who you are and who you ***Will Be***.

Jesus is alive and his spirit is calling you to be betrothed to an everlasting covenant. In this whirlwind romance, you will grow in learning and yearning for the constant presence of Creator God's peace, joy, and hope. Engagement is the trait you must start with. You must engage yourself daily with perfect love and absolute provision.

You do not have to say "yes." You do not have to say "no." Silently accept the offer in timid excitement.

. . . "Just wait and see what's in store for us."

CHAPTER 21

TRAIT 2—PARTICIPATION

ONCE YOU HAVE MADE THE DECISION TO BE ENGAGED with Jesus in this life, in this day, it begins the process of growth, fulfillment, and enlightening. In this daily process of choice, you are now called to join something greater than yourself. You are now part of something more.

You are a part of this Jesus Purpose, but you can only receive its earthly blessings by actively taking part in the actions of love, the giving of grace, in every single thing you do. This is not an unreasonable expectation to hit some magic mark. You have no obligation to meet any standards. You are called to jump all in and continuously get, grow, and give love.

It is an unending cycle of participation.

Our current generation has access to amazing means to connect, share information, and grow in our knowledge bases. These digital tools, while amazingly resourceful, can distract us from the task of participation in any given moment. When improperly applied to our lives, they tend to draw us away from a focus of love and into a closed-structure environment devoid of personal interaction, investment, and achievement.

As an enthusiastic sports fan, I find great enjoyment in watching the unpredictable world of competitive games. I have my personal favorite sports and teams, but truth be told, if the game is good I will watch almost anything. I love seeing the application of preparation, cohesiveness, action, reaction, desire, targets hit, goals attained, and fully engaged participation in live execution.

Sports takes a capable individual or group of individuals and unifies them by a commonly desired outcome. Whether working toward or against each other, the only way to have the possibility for achievement is through collective participation. As the old saying goes, "You have to be in it to win it." You can show up, you can even put on a uniform and still only spectate. Unless you participate in the action of the contest, you are nothing more than an outside observer.

As part of experiencing the Jesus Purpose, we must jump into the middle of the action, so to speak. Despite the tests and conflicts that are certain to be ahead, you have to get down and dirty in activity and the inner workings of love. Love is the playing field you were created to experience and thrive within, it is the ultimate goal of this lived-in tournament you are to achieve victory through.

Participation is the next step beyond engagement. Participation takes what you offer and makes you into a part of something more, and in so, it creates for you an owned share of the outcome. It is where the value of the engagement is now experienced and shared, where *real* life happens.

Inside the Church there are many examples of behavior that draw us into this spirit of participation. We gather together on Sundays. We sing songs of celebration and worship to our Creator God. Jesus directed us to actively take part (participate) in the two unique customs: the Lord's Supper and baptism.

Often called Communion, the Lord's Supper or Eucharist is the breaking of bread and drinking of wine, a tradition which Jesus established at his last meal with his closest followers. Jesus called the bread his body and he called the wine his blood. It's an odd ritual, but an important one. This importance is not about the theological aspects of what Communion is, but rather about the words of Jesus during this special meal with his closest friends.

Jesus asked them to take part in this breaking of bread and drinking of wine in remembrance of him. This was to become a physical exercise of repetition. To "re-" (as in repeatedly) join him in union as a "member" of this newly revealed purpose of love and grace. It allows us to commit and recommit to him in active participation with him and his church.

It is an interactive symbol of our participation in life with Jesus. It is the exchange of personally intimate thoughts and feelings through Body, Mind, and Spirit. We become united into the community of the Jesus Purpose, having shared ownership, responsibility, joys, and inheritance. In this communion we act as one with Jesus to find hope and purpose in this life's journey for what each new day might bring.

Through participation with Jesus and the Church, we get to experience a love that exists beyond ordinary human self-nature. We are lifted from our own natural state and we're able to understand provision on a new level. We recognize the value of life's brokenness and know the awe inspiring power of perfect grace.

When we are a part of this communion of love, we are enabled to grow in God's spirit of love and we begin to understand that He wants what is best for us. From this new perspective we are given access to everything He is and we begin to live forever, starting now.

We become prepared to grow in our own recognition of the value we really hold to Him. We no longer see an imperfect, distorted view through the blurred lens of a broken world. You now become equipped to see through the eyes of a perfect Creator who sees you as His child. He wants to grow with you, invest in who you are now and who you ***Will Be***.

In this process of getting and growing in love, something dynamic takes place. You become over-filled with these understandings and cannot help but to have them expressed as a part of who you are. You are now a vessel of love and you give love-in-action through your interactions. We become inadequate parts of a flawless plan, perfectly placed to share love and taste the fruits of an eternal existence.

We commune in love. We participate with Jesus.

Our participation in this social exercise requires the proper tools of communication to be effective. God gives us prayer, fasting, and the collected canon of the Bible to communicate with us. While, from a surface appearance, prayer is a unidirectional flow of information from us to Him, this is not the intended nature of this communication medium.

Prayer is not simply engaged by bowing heads, closing eyes, and speaking to that which is not seen. Prayer is a connection conduit that is established from spirit to spirit. It is a bidirectional flow of transmission and reception between two tightly linked parties.

We can focus our prayers in moments of meditation, but the purpose of prayer is unceasing. We live in constant prayer with the Spirit of love, who takes up and gives relief from the weights of life, the burdens of bearing, the tolls of shame and anxiety. Prayer is not words from lips or tongues, but connected spirits sharing in the power of love, mercy, and hope.

Through fasting, a component of growing closer to God's love, we are not asked to give up that which we are sustained by, for punishment purposes, but rather to enlighten our lives with the revelation of His daily provisions being overwhelmingly better than anything we can know—including the most basic of necessities like food and drink.

I love food, and if the gospel accounts are accurate, so did Jesus. Jesus was accused of being a glutton and a drunkard. Yet when Jesus needed to strengthen His spirit, he would fast. In yet another counterintuitive picture, we are strengthened not through our own means or willpower, but rather through our weaknesses, developing further understanding and recognition of His love and provision for us as being sufficient for all we need.

Fasting is not about starvation. It is about feeding our spirits through the power of prayer's divine interface. In the accounts of Jesus and his followers, we can observe, relate to, and test these promises of participation.

Participation is about being all in with Jesus.

Jesus really only asked us to participate in two things: Communion, as already noted, and baptism.

Of these odd customs that Jesus specifically indicated have value, the second involves the immersion of one's self in water. This symbolic cleansing has wonderful parallels to being washed clean of sin, being dead and raising in new life, and putting on the image of Jesus. In the simplest of pictures, it is a personal declaration of being all in, totally immersed with Jesus.

Jesus asked us to, in Communion, be all in, wholly participating in life with the "We" God . . . Father-Son-Spirit. To know purpose, is to know Jesus. To live purpose, is to participate daily in the Creator God's unending love and provision for this part of your forever-life.

CHAPTER 22

TRAIT 3—SELFLESSNESS

I JUST SPENT THE PAST WEEK USING MY ACCRUED vacation time to sweat profusely at Camp Ho Non Wah on Wadmalaw Island in coastal South Carolina for my son's Boy Scout Summer Camp experience. For six days with minimal comforts of the civilized world, I volunteered to help "monitor" twenty young men between the ages of eleven to fourteen. It was an overall enjoyable experience outside of the blistering 100-plus-degree temperatures, compounding levels of humidity, and spiders the size of softballs (literally).

I have been dwelling on this third trait for some time prior to sitting down and putting fingers to keyboard, attempting to wrap my own mind around this question: What is selflessness all about?

I had written down the traits as listed several weeks ago as this book was coming more into order. These five traits were my key elements of how I have come to know, accept, and thrive in this discovered and experienced Jesus Purpose.

That stated, I had not broken down into each trait until it came time to write. The first two trait chapters came easily, although what manifested in form was not initially what I had expected. Those chapters almost seemed to write themselves.

This next trait, selflessness, had me a bit stumped.

It seemed too easy to define and process; "Think more about others and less about yourself." Was that all there is to it? Was it really so simple? After all, that is what the world has made out selflessness to mean.

The everyday thoughts of selflessness are summed up in the ideals of generosity and giving: taking what you have been blessed with and sharing it altruistically with others. In a humble benevolence, we are called in religious faith to be compelled to give everything away and follow Jesus.

This mindset is a foundational component of the religious church structure with the rituals of tithes and offerings. Offering one-tenth of what you have into submission for God and sacrificially offering your possessions and resources to His needs. This easily becomes a process of philanthropic competition among individuals and/or groups, attempting to prove who loves God more or gain influence by advertising how much they give away in the name of virtuous sacrifice.

We're shown and taught that selflessness is about how much you contribute versus how little you gain in return. Selflessness has become an equation of faithfulness, a public barometer of how much you love God.

Is that all there is to it? Is it really so simple, so shallow?

I heard a quote of a quote while at summer camp from a young, but wise, staffer. He was summing up an entire semester's college divinity class into a phrase, and it resonated with me:

"Words have usage, not meaning."

This book has beat around that point without articulating it so concisely. Words are used and their meanings need to be leveraged in a means which provide them with the context that gives them the power that provides life and purpose.

Selflessness is not so simple, not so shallow. There is so much more depth to it.

In order to understand selflessness, we must first understand "self."

What is "self"? Self is a perception. We're back to that internalized point of view of your own awareness, processing mechanisms, and understood capabilities. Self is who you see you as.

But, your "self" is not all of who you are or are becoming. Your identity of self is incomplete and corrupted. It is framed within the confines of a broken and limited world. You are not all of who you are, can be, or ***Will Be***.

Self is not the whole picture of you.

The world wants us to believe that "self" is the whole picture of someone. Modern philosophy and culture have elevated the status of self-identity above almost all other things. If you self-believe that you are something, regardless of the testable conditions, you can become or define yourself as such. This is far from truth or reality. Placing such blind value and trust in one's self is equally incomplete and corrupted.

By undermining the very understanding of "self," we relegate selflessness to the act of giving the incomplete and corrupt that only that broken "self" has to offer. This process only yields an outcome of burnout, frustration, and resentment for the giver and its recipients. Its façade of good intentions is supported by a weak and fragile framework of selfishness and narcissism, a hollow infrastructure with emptiness and outfacing vanity as its primary characteristics.

True selflessness—Jesus Purpose selflessness—is not about who you believe you are. In fact, it's about *knowing* you are way more than you believe you are. Selflessness is about developing a core understanding that you are and will become more than you can ever imagine. It's about putting aside the incomplete and corrupted version that only you can see, and replacing it with what you really are. Selflessness is recognizing the "you" that your Creator intended, seeing "you" as Jesus sees you.

This is the intended purpose of selflessness.

At summer camp, I had the opportunity to spend some amazing, quality time with my twelve-year-old son. I know him well. I have frankly known him longer than he has known his "self." I know his strengths and weaknesses. I know his desires and passions, fears and intimidations. He is a part of me and I am part of his very creation. I play an active role in his young life, investing and guiding him through these impressionable years.

I see in him things that he cannot see in himself, glimpses of the man he will become, capacity for greatness that he knows not yet. His self-image is ignorant to these traits. He may never come to know his fullest potential, not because I was wrong, but because this world is finite and limiting.

Your Creator feels the exact same way about you and me.

When we become aware of our "self" and begin to deny that image and understand that we are valued and destined for the limitless, we know in faith that we can have more of Jesus's perspective alive within us. It is then that we connect to Jesus's point of view via the Holy Spirit, and we can have more selflessness.

It is by the very love of Jesus's selflessness that you have been given the blessing to know true freedom, so it is through the action of selflessness that you may in turn choose to love freely!

Then, as we learn to love freely, we are no longer giving of ourselves, but rather from a Creator who has no limits. We can give from His provision of endless resources, filled with an ever-flowing joy and a renewed perspective of becoming more of who we ***Will Be***.

CHAPTER 23

TRAIT 4—GRATITUDE

IF YOU HAVE THE OPPORTUNITY TO READ THIS BOOK, you need to understand how overwhelmingly blessed you are. Not that this book is the blessing, but rather the blessing is the opportunity to have the freedom and ability to read it.

We often live in our own confined worlds of perception, sheltering our awareness from the insensible reality that exists just outside the bounds of our own sightlines. We are cognizant of the darkness and evils that hide in the shadows of those domains—the perversion, the pain, the famine, the brokenness, the wretchedness. They are realities of our world. We do our best to keep them at arm's length or beyond.

These real-life iniquities are harbingers of the chaotic freedom this world constantly chooses; a result from our collective, fallen state of law. They are the heralds of human's conditional state of terminal brokenness. We attempt to hide these sicknesses in the notorious alleys of our societies and turn our attention toward things that we take comfort in. This behavior is not inherently bad. It is how we cope with the hard-to-deal-with truths of a world fallen, yet on course for a destined, divine purpose.

The concept of gratitude is not new to the world, but its foundations are wholly rooted in the infrastructures of faith.

The quality or state of being as "full of thanks" is not a natural characteristic. Rather, our instinctual response, often confused with gratitude, is indebtedness.

Indebtedness is reactionary. It is a behavior based on a sense of obligation. Much too often our responses of thankfulness are caused by this process of motivated indebtedness. This behavior is simply the common exchange of mutually equivalent consideration. It is a mechanical process of reciprocal offerings being traded.

We give these tokens of "appreciation" in a point-of-sale practice. The idea of purchase or sale involves the transfer between two parties of equally valued resources, and this pattern of behavior happens in all areas of our lives, all of the time. Again, this behavior is not inherently bad. It is merely how we are wired as self-focused beings.

As a young man, I was raised to be vigilantly aware of opening doors in public for other people, especially women. It was an expectation that if there was a door, I should book-foot to it and hold it open for the oncoming entrants. It became a source of pride and belief of duty to honor people in this simple, but powerful expression of servanthood. What first began as a behavior of force, turned into a practice of kindness. As a by-product of this simple offering, I would almost always be given a sincere thank-you from those who passed through.

There is an exchange of mutual respect and appreciation for the actions of decency and reverence. The words of thanks in return, while genuine and sincere, were given in this point-of-sale exchange. A give-and-take of respect, they were offered in a spirit of sincere indebtedness, not genuine gratitude.

When we think of our actions and thoughts of appreciation and thankfulness, it may become rather disheartening to recognize how much of these interactions are actually point-of-sale exchanges. Almost all of how we express our appreciation is based on this self-focused mechanism.

Gratitude stands apart from this reactive process. Gratitude has an ingrained relationship with grace. It is a proactive state-of-being. The root words of gratitude and grace come from the same place, having meanings that tie back before their obvious Latin heritage. These words combine the unnatural ideas of acceptance, lovingness, and praise. They offer a glimpse into the supernatural part of who we are created to be: accepted, loved, and pardoned.

Gratitude encompasses more than a feeling; it is a by-product from being grounded in an eternally focused state of mind. Gratitude is understanding that our indebtedness can never be equitable to the forgiveness and compassion offered to us; that there is no means for us to ever, in any point-of-sale exchange, provide any comparable means of payment or reciprocation to the price that has already been paid. It is part of a transition from a lifestyle of recognition and understanding toward acknowledgement.

Gratitude as a state of mind comes from *knowing* with confidence that you are accepted, loved, and pardoned through Jesus.

I'm not sure we can truly understand gratitude without Jesus, but I believe we can get close. When we observe and contemplate the sacrifices made from others for our benefit, we can experience moments and instances of true gratitude. We can draw a direct connection to the realization our indebtedness has no means to be repaid. These perspectives draw sincere and real emotions from within us; but they are only reflections of the finite reality which life in this broken world offers.

Feelings of thanks and indebtedness are limited to this world. Living in a state of eternal gratitude must therefore transcend this world.

When we strive to become the trait of gratitude, we cannot help but offer our lives into the purpose of grace—they are, after all, intimately related. Through our acknowledgement of grace, we become aware of the unpayable indebtedness we are given and choose to offer our lives to others and to our Creator God without any expectation of repayment.

This is where grace meets love. Our self-focused state is to look for the reciprocation of appreciation. Jesus offers his grace to the entire world without expectancy.

His love is no different toward those who recognize and accept it than to those who do not. There is no expectation of any debt to be repaid. The gratitude trait causes us who do choose to accept and follow Jesus to change, to transition from our self-focused state to a love-focused state. This change is not out of any obligation or indebtedness, but out of our spirit's growth and strengthening.

As our Spirit connects more closely with the understanding of how amazing this grace is, we cannot help but become aware of God's love for us, and the more grateful and full of grace we become. This state of being spills over from within our spirits into our minds and out of our bodies. It allows others to be impacted by love in a way that is far from natural. We become powered by that which is supernatural.

We no longer look for repayment, offering our lives as a part of the Jesus Purpose. We draw in line with a love-focused yearning to have others understand and know this supernatural peace and perspective. The idea of sacrifice changes from a sense of moral obligation to a compelling of burning selfless desire.

We become and ***Will Be*** a life that manifests itself as a living testament, an active example of eternal hope.

CHAPTER 24

TRAIT 5—HOPE

VERY EARLY IN THIS BOOK I MENTIONED THAT IF YOU met me, you'd probably think that I am a guy who really loves life. That statement is still true. I do love life. I love living life!

I strongly believe that every moment, each breath and heartbeat is a gift. Whether you are aware or inclined enough to test this Jesus Purpose, it all comes down to this trait of hope. To properly understand your blessings, wrap your heart around the concept of grace, and find a new perspective to filter this creation through, you have to know Jesus.

Hope is yet another unnatural human trait. Hope should not exist. If we look at our lives and world from reality disconnected from the possible connection to a personally relevant Creator, what should we expect from the absolute future? You are running a race away from an imminent death. It will catch you. This is the certainty of life. There is no opportunity to escape this outcome. There are no magic tricks or alternate means to avoid the course of your destiny. It is coming.

So what?

It's often a common exercise among people who are seeking purpose and fulfillment in their lives to ask the question, "What would you do today if you knew you would die tomorrow?" This question is intended to awaken the atrophied and decaying recesses of our mind and spirits. It is a reveille's call to reinvigorate the fading aspects of a life trapped in purposeless behaviors, routines developed in a mindset of survival, a built-up callous on the minds and hearts of people who do not know the true wonder of love and grace.

This question often leads people to fulfill their unaccomplished earthly desires. Some chase the feats of the extreme, like skydiving while laughing in the face of the fragility of life, acting for the first time without fear of what is unavoidable. Others will cling to family and close friends, investing in the personal relationships which have brought these temporary tastes of true joy and peace. Yet others will spend the question in contemplation, desperately seeking any means of prolonging time before the certainty ahead, spending all remaining resources in attempts to survive one more precious moment.

This entire Jesus Purpose, the whole point of our life is to be freed from the burden of death. Knowing Jesus is knowing hope. The question "What would you do today if you knew you would die tomorrow?" is the wrong question to ask if what Jesus offers is real.

The question changes to "What would you do today if you knew you would never die?" How would you change what you think, how you react, how you observe? If you could know with trust and confidence that tomorrow is the beginning of a life that cannot be extinguished, what would you do today?

What if you were offered a way to wake up every morning in a state of awe and wonder; overwhelmed at the gift of another breath in the provision of a Creator's love? If your interactions with others were filtered through a lens of a grace to proactively offer abundant mercy and kindness to <u>all</u> people? What if you were filled with an assuredness that nothing can change the course of eternity you are on; to claim and champion a victory in forever-joy and peace; to live, right now, without fear or worry as a personal trait? What if you were allowed to experience time without end, starting today?

Knowing Jesus is knowing hope. Hope is not natural and cannot be naturally acquired. Many other faith perspectives and religions offer tastes of hope. They provide insight to truths within this testable world which are difficult to deny. Every other life perspective aside from the Jesus Purpose falls into one or more of three possible categories: Law, Natural, and Spiritual.

Law is a perspective that makes the claims that there are thresholds of attainment which you can personally achieve. There are rules and regulations through which, if you abide by them, you can know hope.

Natural perspectives claim all that has been, is, and will be exists for itself. There is little purpose aside from happenstance. In its essence, a natural perspective seeks one common requirement, an essential factor to make its claims and perspective bulletproof. To have what little hope can be found in this type of mindset, to know that this life really is an inconsequential existence, the infinite must somehow exist outside what is finite.

Spiritual perspectives claim that we are not subjected to this life in this realm without a purpose beyond the measurable, and that within each of us there is a life beyond the physical. Through a process of reincarnation and enlightenment, you must fabricate your own eternal hope and peace apart from what created you.

These alternate perspectives on life yield limited results. Elements of love, peace, understanding, and truth can be accessed through their offerings. Commonly though, they all fail to offer one simple factor: certainty.

No other life perspective ever conceived offers the certainty that the Jesus Purpose offers. With law, you must be above the minimum rung of the legal ladder to reach eternity. With the natural, you require that which is infinite, conceptual, and untestable. With the spiritual, you are wholly responsible to find the lonely path to attain that which has no clear definition. In all these faith perspectives, your faith is placed squarely on you. You must have complete hope and faith in yourself.

This is the choice of the Jesus Purpose:

There are no magic words. There is no pixie dust, and there is no ulterior motive. The law directs us to need the grace Jesus offers. The natural points us to need the infinite Jesus offers. The spiritual calls us to the destination Jesus offers.

These perspectives of mankind's making are not absent from love, peace, understanding, and truth. They are beckoning you to be satisfied. They are calling you to your purpose. Are you satisfied? Do you know, with certainty, that hope is real?

You have a choice. This decision is not offered in anger, wrath, bigotry, or divisiveness. This decision does not come with a book of "small-print legalese" which must be notarized, verified, and filed away like a Monopoly get-out-of-jail-free card. This decision is not an instantaneous flip of a switch to a life of candy and roses.

This decision is about finding and knowing hope . . . realizing what you ***Will Be.***

What would you do today if you knew you would never die?

In love, with grace and freedom, you can know the purpose Jesus has for you, or you can go it alone.

Knowing Jesus is knowing hope.

CHAPTER 25

THE ANSWER, ***<u>WILL BE</u>***

THROUGH THE JESUS PURPOSE, ENGAGEMENT, PARTNERship, selflessness, gratitude, and hope are who you ***<u>Will Be</u>***.

You have likely noticed the not-so-subtle combination of **bold**, *italicized*, and <u>underlined</u> references to this odd pair of words continued throughout the course of this wandering stream-of-thought journey. The combination of these three intensifying font-factors and two small words are the answer to every question about why you are, who you are.

The following perspective is likely one of the most challenging, poorly recognized, and misunderstood aspects of the Jesus Purpose. Very little is offered from our culture on the truth of what is to be revealed in this chapter. Yet, in our Creator's unending wisdom, it is how He offered Himself in introduction to us.

I'm sure you have encountered the phrase "lost in translation." In our world of multilingual, culturally diverse people, we can often miss the behind-the-scenes relevance when something is translated between languages or cultures.

Even in a shared, common-language conversation, words can only convey so much in their raw state. Without proper context and point of view, confusion happens easily and often.

As a married man I can attest, with the utmost confidence, that interpersonal communication is HARD!

"No, I don't have any clue what you are referencing when you say, 'thingumajig,' honey."

"You are saying you're not mad at me, but everything else you're doing says you are."

Even within the most tight-knit interpersonal partnerships, misunderstandings often occur. This is completely normal and part of how you were designed. It requires effort, lots and lots of effort, to know someone and care enough to dig past the surface message of what is being said, and to desperately desire the truth that resides past what the words offered actually mean.

In this adventure of engagement and partnership, this is where we are called to journey, to travel into a place which may be slightly uncomfortable and difficult to rationalize, but which offers a depth of relevance that cannot be restrained.

What is ***Will Be***?

You have likely heard God's name referenced as "I Am that I Am" or "I Am." It is directly connected to the Old Testament account of Moses and his first personal encounter with the Creator God of his ancestors. He asked God for His name, and this is how it is often translated into our language and culture.

But this is actually a mistranslation. We have lost a key detail in the process.

The verb tense of the name God uses is not in the present. Instead, God, the self-identified Creator, gives His personal name in a future-tense: "I ***Will Be*** that which I ***Will Be.***"

This subtle adjustment makes a significant difference when we begin to develop a perspective that God is seeking a forever-focused partnership with us. That His purpose with you is affixed not on the moment that is and is now in the past, but God is forever-fixated ahead of where you are. He is where you ***Will Be***.

He is already there with you.

Your Creator ***Will Be*** there to provide for you. He ***Will Be*** there for you, comforting, healing, laughing, renewing, counseling, loving, and providing perfect grace. In this name He has planned for not who you are, but for who you ***Will Be*** in eternity with Them, Father, Son, and Spirit. It solidifies the concept and promise of partnership in today and to come. ***Will Be*** is who ***God*** is with ***You***.

You cannot become who you were intended to be without a partnership with God.

Earlier in this book, a notion was given that you are not equal to anyone, that you as a creation are as individual as your fingerprint is. No one will ever have your perspective, your thoughts, and your experiences. You are completely individual. This idea of your uniqueness is central to the life-changing importance of ***Will Be***.

Just as no one will have your perspective, no other human will have the exclusive partnership you share with your Creator God—no one, not even Jesus.

You as ***Will Be*** and the God named ***Will Be*** will have a union and a name that cannot be understood by any other mind, body, or spirit. In the new creation, upon your marriage with perfect grace, you will have a name written for you, to which only you and the "We" God will be able to translate and understand.

Jesus has that same exact relationship with God. He has a name written that only "They" can translate and understand within the perfect union of their "We" partnership.

Through Jesus, you are invited into that same level of personally invested, mutually beneficial relationship with your Creator; a perfect marriage, an eternal partnership of perfect communion.

This is the answer to who you ***Will Be***.

Conclusion

THIS BOOK HAS BEEN JUST OVER A YEAR IN THE MAKING. The ideas and thoughts offered are not dogmatic; they are not to be treated as doctrine or prophecy. This is not a book which intends to create conflict or divisiveness. It is a calling of redemption, a praise of hope and purpose that I passionately desire to share with so many.

This world, this culture of disconnection we are enabling, is yearning for reformation. There is an obvious desperation for real life and real hope. I see it everywhere.

I observe a widening divide between the collective Church and its commissioned purpose. I observe the title of Christian carrying disdain in those who most desperately need the love and grace we are called to openly and lavishly give. I observe the polarization of politics, zealots of control becoming empowered as we willingly yield our freedoms into their throngs of earthly regulation. I observe an ever-growing population of believers in themselves, a corporate brainwashing of limited self-satisfaction and dead-end profiteering. I observe global atrocities, personal hatred, senseless violence, purity's perversion, and uninterrupted heartache and tragedy. I observe the race of humanity in need of the answers to all of these trials as never before. A solution is being freely offered, yet has never before been more overwhelmed amongst the noise of ever-active surroundings which drown out the quiet calling of each life's true purpose.

We all have a choice. We all have an opportunity to change our minds. We all have an opportunity to know with confidence. We all have an opportunity to yield our desires for control and power. We all have an opportunity to live engaged, partnered, selfless, grateful, and hope-filled lives.

This existence is a test, a test of freedom and love, and you have done nothing to earn the hope it can offer. You do not have to wait to know who you were created to become.

Seek Jesus.

Really . . . Go, now. See if what he offers is real.

Find Jesus. Test Jesus. Get to know Jesus.

Discover who he is and what he said and what he did and is for you. Journey this adventure with him. Learn his way and his truth, and find a real, abundant, fulfilling love which fills the void of emptiness in this world, in your life.

In Purpose, with Jesus, you ***Will Be*** made alive and you forever ***Will Be*** . . .

About the Cover

In the spring of 2008, I had the pleasure of teaching what has become my favorite series to share. It is an eight-week, in-depth study on the last week of Jesus's earthly life, focusing on the time just before and through his crucifixion, death, and resurrection.

This is not your typical Easter Bible Study. We dig deep within historical prophecy, Jewish tradition and culture, and the associated parallels of written documentation. It seeks to provide what I have always called "Faith Reinforcement," a strengthening of trust in who and why Jesus is someone we can and should believe in. This study takes the accounts of Jesus and his last eye-witnessed actions and highlights the astounding associations with who he claimed to be and why he is our life's purpose.

After one night's lesson on the Roman crucifixion process, I fell into conversation with a good friend who happens to be a magnificent artist. His name is Marlan Yoder, and his spiritual journey is an amazing story within itself. Growing up as Anabaptist Mennonites, he and his beautiful wife Cheryl sought for a more engaging relationship with their known Creator. Through their travels and trials, they were brought to His Hands to be a foundational part of our church family.

Marlan's renowned artwork shifted to a passion and an intense focus on the Tree of Life, a powerful and ever-present symbol that His Hands Church uses often. I doubt Marlan could even tell you how many trees he has painted in the past ten years. His tree paintings of all shapes, shades, and depths line the church's corridors. They have become an ingrained part of our culture and help reinforce the heart of our church's purpose, to love people to Jesus.

In our intimate moment of connection after my teaching session, our dialog moved through and past the traditional imagery of Jesus's execution. The "low tau" or "lowercase-t" Roman cross is the typical version of what we have been shown in most religious artwork and depiction, and based on the historical understandings of Jesus's particular execution, it still seems the most likely fit. However, in this moment of discussion we opened the door to other, less likely, but still plausible alternatives to this traditional imagery.

One of these alternative cross options suggests that Jesus was hung on the trunk of a tree with his crossbar suspended, securing his nail-pierced hands with outstretched arms. This cross-member would have been the item he and the Samaritan carried to the place of the skull, Golgotha. A simple plank of aged wood affixed to a living, vertical fixture already in place. The Romans were experts in public humiliation and civic killings, and they would have wasted little resources in their slaying endeavors of any condemned common person. They saved the iron from the nails, repurposing them for the next wave of public victims. It seems unlikely to me that they would waste much effort in installing three vertical shafts just for the routine punishments of Jesus and the other two rebellious offenders of that now infamous day.

A tree trunk or a preexisting wooden structure seems the way the machine of Rome would have operated from a mere efficiency standpoint. It was also customary that those convicted and sentenced to death be displayed near the location of the arrest. Jesus was arrested in the Garden of Gethsemane located on the Mount of Olives, where ancient olive trees are still in place.

Please realize this is not a traditional perspective, but a connecting concept of faith, purpose, and love. Period historians would probably lean toward other, more traditional views, but Marlan and I were not having a historical discussion. This was a spiritual discussion, investigating the bigger picture of God's perfect plan of freedom, love, and grace. We were looking from before the beginning, through and past the finite end which is coming. We were collectively realizing that it is all perfectly aligned through this moment in time and space—the moment of Jesus's life-giving sacrifice.

No matter if this structure that Jesus was nailed to was an actual tree, it was undoubtedly the Tree of Life.

The image of Jesus on the cross is the fulfillment and purpose of the very first human encounter with God in the Garden of Eden. We were called to live at the Tree of Life, where our brokenness and death is vanquished forever, and perfect mercy is offered without pretense.

All we are asked to do is accept this as truth.

Through this conversation, I believe Marlan's artist's-eye was opened to a new and freeing image of what Jesus's sacrifice was revealing: the true completion of creation's purpose and love. The real Tree of Life.

One week after our conversation, Marlan brought the painting you see on the cover of this book to our church and showed it to me. He said he could not get our conversation out of his mind and had to paint what he was shown by the Holy Spirit. On the back of the handcrafted piece, along the framework of the tightly stretched canvas, was a small note written, "Thanks for the inspiration, Bill."

This painting hangs right across from the doorway of the prayer room in His Hands Church. I am still overwhelmed at the goodness and love of God through others at times.

Marlan is an introverted deep thinker and I am an unabashed, *extroverted* deep thinker. But for a moment, despite our easily noticed personality mismatch, we connected beyond tradition and religion. Between the spaces of reality, time, and mystery, in our deep-thinking talk, we basked in the revelation of divine truth and spirit-connected, everlasting life.

Ever since Marlan showed me our Tree of Life painting, a low-resolution photo has been the staple background image of my cell phone, something that I hold and view almost daily. It has become a personal reminder of the perfect plan that God has for me and others around me.

When this book began to take form and substance, I really struggled with what the cover would look like. How intense should it be? What kind of depth should it have?

I knew the title from the start. It was bold and direct, intentionally so. I wanted readers to be challenged that someone might have the audacity to succinctly connect Jesus to the purpose of life. It is not the first, nor last, written linking of these two concepts, but I believe it may be the most simply stated and personally poignant.

I was more hesitant with the idea of the cover art, but my gorgeous wife, Kristina, from the moment she helped refine the early rough drafts, clearly knew that Marlan's Tree of Life painting was meant to be the cover. She could see the painting and its future impact as a key part of *The Jesus Purpose*.

This is a wonderful image of transitioning partnership, moving through the processes of God's perfect plans all together, and working for years to complete an outcome beyond what any of us could have imagined. I asked Marlan for permission to use the piece, and he graciously offered it . . . without pretense.

There was one caveat however. As a professional artist, Marlan makes a living from his artwork and reprints of his artwork. Often when someone cannot afford an original or when the personal value is too strong to sell, Marlan will allow a high-resolution, photographed reprint of his painting to be made and sold.

In some unintended manner, this Tree of Life painting had never been properly captured for reprint. Mind you, this was not for lack of request. Just two years ago, right before the diagnosis of her brain aneurysm, Kristina requested a print of this painting for my Christmas present, but Marlan could not provide it because it had not yet been professionally photographed. It was as if the recapturing of this unique image was being unintentionally delayed for a more purposeful future moment.

In the continuing cycle of transitioning this partnership of purpose, we engaged with another dear friend and fixture at His Hands, an amazing photographer named Tom Mileshko. I asked Tom, with permission from Marlan, if he could help us capture the distinctive essence of this incredible, one-of-a-kind painting. He also humbly offered his time and service . . . without pretense.

The creation of this book cover was an assembly of normal people with extraordinary talents offering themselves for a collective good beyond themselves. This is the model of loving through Christ, the mission of the church—getting, growing, and giving God's love . . . without pretense.

I am honored and blessed to call these my friends and partners in this process. I am so grateful that they will forever be a part of my God story; a story about Jesus, about purpose, and about finding the true Tree of Life.

Learn more about Marlan Yoder at marlanyoderart.com
Learn more about Tom Mileshko Photography at milepix.com
Learn more about His Hands Church at hishandschurch.com

ABOUT THE AUTHOR

WILLIAM THRASHER IS A UNIQUELY ORDINARY GUY; A life-taught academic and a warrior who is at peace. Through experience, study, and prayer, William has found an amazing outlook on life and its ultimate purpose. He has a burning desire to share his story and its life-changing insight with everyone.

A US Marine, husband, father, and lover of life, William is also a passionate teacher gifted with a unique perspective and a skilled leader in the field of business. As an author, public speaker, and college minister he has a true passion to share his path to knowing hope and peace, a journey he has personally endeavored.

Raised inside the culture of the westernized evangelical church, William has broken free of traditional religion rules and believes in the good news of God's unbounded love and grace for humanity. William has a gifted understanding of the balance required for finding hope, peace, and purpose.

William Thrasher lives in Woodstock, GA, with his wife Kristina, son Will, daughter Ainsleigh, and pound puppy Bubbles. Active in the community, William works with His Hands Church, the Marine Corps League, Boy Scouts of America, and other outreach missions. He has professionally advanced through the ranks of the commercial audiovisual industry for the past seventeen years, and is currently the Vice President of Operations at AV-Tech Media Solutions, headquartered in Roswell, GA. William, a supernaturally-gifted roller-skater, enjoys attending Georgia Tech football games, listening to great music, watching Marvel superhero movies, playing outdoors, spending quality time with his family, and loving this adventure called life.

For more information about *The Jesus Purpose* and its author, please visit our website, *thejesuspurpose.com*.